Ryszard Kapuściński was born in 1932 in Pinsk in eastern Poland. He was educated in Warsaw and at the age of twenty-three was posted to India, his first trip outside Poland. His first book, *The Polish Bush*, stories of the Polish 'frontier', appeared in 1962 and was an immediate bestseller. He since travelled widely throughout the Third World – storing up, as he once said in an interview, the experiences for the books that would come later. The first of these books, published in 1968, was based on a journey through Islamic Russia. This was followed by books on Africa, Latin America and South Africa. His first book to be translated into English was *The Emperor*, based on the last days of Haile Selassie and subsequently made into a play produced by Jonathan Miller. His other books in English include *Another Day of Life*, about the war in Angola, and *Shah of Shahs*, based on the Revolution in Iran. He is also the author of the highly acclaimed *Imperium*, the story of his travels across the dying empire of the Soviet Union in 1989, which is also published by Granta Books. Ryszard Kapuściński died in Warsaw in January 2007, at the age of seventy-four.

The Soccer War

Ryszard Kapuściński

Translated from the Polish by William Brand

Afterword by Bill Buford

Granta Books
London

Granta Publications, 2/3 Hanover Yard, Noel Road, London N1 8BE

First published in Great Britain by Granta Books, 1990
This edition published by Granta Books, 2007

A CIP catalogue record for this book
is available from the British Library.

3 5 7 9 10 8 6 4 2

Printed and bound in Great Britain by
CPI Bookmarque, Croydon

Mixed Sources
Product group from well-managed
forests and other controlled sources
www.fsc.org Cert no. TT-COC-002227
© 1996 Forest Stewardship Council
FSC

CONTENTS

Acknowledgements

The quotation from *Tristes Tropiques* (London, 1973, translated by John and Doreen Weigh) on Page 142 is reprinted by kind permission of Jonathan Cape Ltd.

THE HOTEL METROPOL

I am living on a raft in a side-street in the merchant district of Accra. The raft stands on pilings, two-storeys high, and is called the Hotel Metropol. In the rainy season this architectural monstrosity rots and festers with mould, and in the dry months it expands at the joints and cracks. But it does not fall apart! In the middle of the raft there is a construction that has been partitioned into eight compartments. These are our rooms. The remaining space, surrounded by a balustrade, is called the veranda. There we have a big table for meals and a few small folding tables where we drink whiskey and beer.

In the tropics, drinking is obligatory. In Europe, the first thing two people say when they meet is 'Hello. What's new?' When people greet each other in the tropics, they say 'What would you like to drink?' They frequently drink during the daytime, but in the evening the drinking is mandatory; the drinking is premeditated. After all, it is the evening that shades into night, and it is the night that lies in wait for anyone reckless enough to have spurned alcohol.

The tropical night is a hardened ally of all the world's makers of whiskey, cognac, liqueurs, schnapps and beers, and the person who denies them their sales is assailed by the night's ultimate weapon: sleeplessness. Insomnia is always wearing, but in the tropics it is killing. A person punished all day by the sun, by a thirst that can't be satisfied, maltreated and weakened, has to sleep.

He has to. And then he cannot!

It is too stuffy. Damp, sticky air fills the room. But then, it's not air. It's wet cotton. Inhale, and it's like swallowing a ball of cotton dipped in warm water. It's unbearable. It nauseates, it prostrates, it unhinges. The mosquitoes sting, the monkeys scream. Your body is sticky with sweat, repulsive to touch. Time stands still. Sleep will not come. At six in the morning, the same invariable six in the morning all year round, the sun rises. Its rays increase the dead steam-bath closeness. You should get up. But you don't have the strength. You don't tie your shoes because the effort of bending over is too much. You feel worn out like an old pair of slippers. You feel used up, toothless, baggy. You are tormented by undefined longings, nostalgias, dusky pessimisms. You wait for the day to pass, for the night to pass, for all of it, damn it to hell, finally to pass.

So you drink. Against the night, against the depression, against the foulness floating in the bucket of your fate. That's the only struggle you're capable of.

Uncle Wally drinks because it does his lungs some good. He has tuberculosis. He is thin, and each breath comes hard, with a wheeze. He takes a seat on the veranda and calls, 'Papa! One!' Papa goes to the bar and brings him a bottle. Uncle Wally's hand starts trembling. He pours some whiskey into the glass and tops it up with cold water. He downs the drink and starts on another. Tears come to his eyes, and he shakes with a voiceless sob. Ruin, waste. He is from London, was a carpenter in England. The war brought him to Africa. He stayed. He is still a carpenter, but he has taken to drink and carries round that battered lung that he never treats. With what could he get treatment? Half his money goes to the hotel, and the other half for whiskey. He has nothing, literally nothing. His shirt is in tatters; his only pair of trousers full of patches; his sandals crumbling. His impeccably elegant countrymen have cursed him and driven him away. They have forbidden him to say that he is English. Dirty lump. Fifty-four years old. What is left for him? Drink a little whiskey and start pushing up daisies.

So he drinks and waits for his shot at the daisies. 'Don't get angry at the racists,' he tells me. 'Don't get all wound up about the bourgeoisie. Do you think they'll plant you in different dirt when your number comes up?'

His love for Ann. My God: love. Ann came around here when she needed money for a taxi fare. Once she had been Papa's girl, demanding her petty compensation—two shillings. Her face was tattooed. She came from the northern tribe of the Nankani, and in the north they canker the faces of their infants. The custom dates from when the southern tribes conquered the northern ones and sold them to the whites as slaves, and so the northerners disfigured their foreheads, cheeks and noses to make themselves unsaleable goods. In the Nankani language the words for ugly and free mean the same thing. Synonyms.

Ann had soft, sensual eyes. All of her was in those eyes. She would look at somebody long and kittenishly, and when she saw her gaze working she would laugh and say, 'Give me two shillings for cab-fare.'

Uncle Wally always came over. He would pour her a whiskey, grow lachrymose and smile. He told her, 'Ann, stay with me and I'll stop drinking. I'll buy you a car.'

She answered, 'What do I need a car for? I prefer to make love.'

He said, 'We'll make love.'

She asked, 'Where?' Uncle Wally got up from his table; it was only a few steps to his room. He opened the door, grasping the handle, trembling. The dark coop contained an iron bed and a small chest.

Ann burst out laughing. 'Here? Here? My love has to live in palaces. In the palaces of the white kings!'

We were watching. Papa went over, tapped Ann on the shoulder and mumbled, 'Shove off.' She left gaily, waving to us—'Bye bye.' Uncle Wally returned to his table. He picked up the bottle as though to drink it straight down in one go, but before he had finished it, he was slumping in his chair. We carried the old desperado into his chicken coop of a room, to the iron bed, and laid him on the white sheet—without Ann.

After that, he told me, 'Red, the only woman who won't betray you is your mother. Don't count on anyone else.' I loved listening to him. He was wise. He told me: 'The African praying mantis is more honest than our wives. Do you know the mantis? Courtships don't last long in the world of the mantis. The insects have their wedding ceremony, leave for the honeymoon, and in the morning the female bites the male to death. Why bother tormenting him for a lifetime? The result is the same, isn't it? And whatever is done more quickly is done more honestly.'

The bitter tone in Uncle Wally's outpourings always disquiets Papa. Papa keeps us on a short leash. Before I go out I have to tell him where I am going and why. Otherwise there will be a scene. 'I worry about you,' Papa screams. When an Arab screams there's no reason to take it seriously. It's just his way of speaking. And Papa is an Arab, a Lebanese. Habib Zacca. He has been leasing the hotel for a year. 'Since the Big Crash,' Papa says. Oh, yes, he got wiped out.

'Zacca?' a friend of his cries, 'Zacca—he was a millionaire. A millionaire! Zacca had a villa, cars, shops, orchards.'

'When my watch stopped, I'd throw it out of the window,' Papa sighs. 'The doors of my house were always open. A crowd of guests every day. Come on in, eat, drink, whatever you want. And now? They don't even say hello. I have to go and present myself to the gluttons who ate and drank me out of thousands.' Papa came to Ghana twenty years ago. He began with a fabric shop and made a great fortune, which he lost afterwards, in a year. He lost it at the races. 'The horses ate me, Red.'

I saw his stables once, in a palm forest outside the city. Nine white horses: splendid Arabs. The way he knew them, the way he stroked them! Papa may have shouted at his wife but with his horses he was as tender as a lover. He led one out. 'The best horse in all Africa,' he said, despairingly, because it had an incurable wound on its pastern. All the horses had wounds of this kind, and the stables were slowly dying out. For him this was a tragedy greater than the loss of millions. Once the horses died, his one passion would go unrequited. There were days when he could not visit the stable, and he became irritable and couldn't be calmed until he was back in the palm forest, watching the stable boys walking past him, leading one swift Arab with bloodshot eyes after another.

Papa never shows his wife the horses. He treats her sharply and unpleasantly. She often sits silent and motionless in a chair, smoking a cigarette. I once asked her, 'How old are you?' 'Twenty-eight,' she answered. But she is as white-haired as a dove, pale and wrinkled. She has borne four children. Two live in Lebanon and two in Accra. Sometimes she brings her daughter along, a sickly, handicapped little girl who throws herself on the floor and creeps around on her hands and knees, screaming. She is ten years old and can't walk or speak. She crawls to a corner where a record-player stands, raises her head and begs with her eyes. The mother puts a record on; Dalida sings and the girl's screams mix with the song. She is happy, her face becomes radiant. The record ends and a moan rises in the girl's throat. She is asking for more.

The little one clings only to the Premier. He alone is able to make her smile. She hugs his legs, fawns on him, purrs. He strokes her head and tugs at her ear. We call him the Premier because he is always dropping the names of acquaintances in the Guinean government. He once lived in Conakry and traded something there. 'If anybody's going to Guinea, just let me know,' he boasts. 'I'll give you a letter to Sekou Touré. My pal. Ministers? Who cares about ministers? Don't waste your time talking to ministers.'

The Premier and I are in cahoots. He takes me aside and buys me a beer. 'Listen, Red,' he begins, 'you've travelled all over the world, so tell me, where can I get a big business going? My operation in Ghana is small-time. Very small-time.'

I look at that fat little man, at his sweaty face and his hangdog expression. What could I tell him? I think to myself: he's a petty capitalist, not a financial shark, another little man in the ranks of the army of little shopkeepers—why not toss him an idea? I ponder: Burma, Japan, Pakistan. Everywhere it's crowded, everywhere there's a crush.

'Maybe India?' the Premier asks.

Oh, no, India's tough. There are monopolies everywhere. 'Too many monopolies,' I say. 'Damned capitalism.'

He nods and admits gloomily, 'Damned capitalism.' The Premier moves from country to country, trying to break into the market, to get off the ground; he has pitched his tent under many skies. Nothing doing. A sterile waste of time, an embittering struggle. 'Isn't there any country for a big business?' he asks.

'Perhaps not,' I say. 'The way I see it, there isn't.'

The Premier walks around, mulling things over, asking the same questions. He bought himself a globe and he runs his fingers over it. He calls me: 'What about here, Red?'

I look. He's pointing to the Philippines.

'Uh, no,' I say. 'The Americans are there.'

'The Americans?' he assures himself with foreboding. 'Only small business, right?'

I show him with my fingers: 'Small for sure. A tiny business.'

He thinks it over for a while and confides: 'I would very much love a big business. More than women.'

'Don't you like women?' I interject.

'Of course. They're good too. Now the most beautiful women are in Dakar.'

On this subject the Premier is always arguing with Young Khouri, the son of Big Khouri (also Lebanese). Nadir, Young Khouri, is a true man of the world. He has a car in London, a car in Paris and another one in Rome. A complete dolt. Talking with him is the summit of amusement for me.

'Come to Australia with me,' he proposes.

'But I don't have any money,' I answer.

'Write to your father. He can send you some.'

'My father's rather tight-fisted,' I explain. 'He won't give me money for a flight to Australia.'

Nadir knows no limits in dissipation and squandering. He has everything. He is always getting cash from his father. Big Khouri loves little Khouri. The old man lives in a small house in a hamlet outside Accra. The house is rotting and the furniture is falling to pieces. A threadbare homestead. Yet it is the residence of perhaps the wealthiest man in all of West Africa, the multimillionaire Big Khouri. This street trader from Beirut has capital but no needs. He eats simple Arab rye bread, baked on a stove, while his profits mount to dizzyingly high sums. He is an old man and could die this year. In Beirut he owns a whole street of houses. He has never seen them.

Big Khouri is illiterate. A confidant writes his business letters, a man who lives with us in the Metropol and to whom Young Khouri always defers. 'He's an intellectual,' he would tell me. Gregarious, witty, the intellectual can

17

shake jokes out of his sleeve. He showed us a photograph of a sweet, old lady under an umbrella. 'This is my fiancée,' he explained. 'She lives in California. She has been waiting for me for fifteen years. She'll wait fifteen more and die. But death isn't so terrible. You just have to be very tired.' And he burst out laughing. The intellectual drank in secret, never on the veranda. He said that drinking in front of others showed lack of culture. In the middle of the conversation he stood up, went to his room and drained a bottle greedily. Then we heard the thud of his body hitting the floor: somehow he never manages to make it to his bed.

When he is not writing letters for Big Khouri, the intellectual argues with Napoleon. Napoleon is a tiny creature with a well-rounded belly. 'I long for home,' Napoleon says. 'I long for home.' But he never budges. He marches round the veranda as though on parade, back and forth. He takes out his mirror and counts his wrinkles. 'I'm sixty, and look how young I am, how strong. I can walk and walk and never get tired. Come on, how old do I look?'

Papa answers, 'Twenty.'

'So, you all see,' Napoleon exalts, pulling in his belly until the veins on his temples bulge. He might have a screw loose. He will go away one day. The sound of his tramping will stop. It will be quieter.

You can see the veranda from the street, illuminated by several weak lightbulbs. By the light, shadows moving along the raft are visible from below. The shadows belong to no one. Their mute pantomime, their slow dance, takes place in the heart of Kokompe. But that quarter, black to the core, does not acknowledge their existence. Kokompe has its own life, foreign and inaccessible to the Metropol. In the opinion of the quarter, the shadows on the raft belong to a different world, one occupied by the bungalows of white administrators and business representatives, the

Cantonments district. That's where you belong, Kokompe says.

But the shadows do not exist in the eyes of the Cantonments either. God forbid! The Cantonments quarter turns its back on the raft with contempt and shame. The raft is a disgrace that the Cantonments prefer to see hushed up. The Cantonments—that rich, elegant, snobbish, bureaucratic, European, bourgeois dame.

So the raft is not hitched to anybody's boat—the shadows exist for themselves. They could multiply or disappear—it wouldn't mean a thing. 'Does anything have meaning?' Uncle Wally asks. Nobody answers him.

How did I end up among the castaways living on the raft? I would certainly never have met them if it had not been for a chance meeting with a young woman who did not desire an Arab.

In 1958 I flew from London to Accra. The airplane was a big, slow BOAC Super Constellation. I set out full of excitement and, at the same time, full of anxiety about what might happen: I knew no one in Ghana, had no names, addresses, contacts and, worst of all, I didn't have much money. I got a window seat; to my right sat an Arab and next to him a fair girl, the Scandinavian type, with a bouquet of flowers on her knees.

We flew across the Sahara at night; such flights are splendid because the airplane seems to be suspended among the stars. Stars overhead—that's understandable. But stars below as well, along the bottom of the night. Why it's so, I can't say.

The Arab was trying to pick up the Scandinavian girl who, it turned out, was flying to her boy-friend (a technician working on a contract with a government firm) and carrying him flowers. But my neighbour wouldn't be deterred: he wanted to propose right there; he promised her a beautiful and elegant life in any part of the world she chose. He assured her that he was rich—he had a lot of money—and he repeated the phrase several times: a lot of money. In the end the Scandinavian, calm and patient at the outset, grew bored, then angry, and then she told him to stop tormenting her, and finally she got up and moved to another seat.

A banal little incident. But with this result: the Arab, slightly demoralized, changed the object of his attention and turned to me. His name was Nadir Khouri. And me?

Such-and-such.

And who was I?

A reporter.

Why was I travelling?

To look, to walk around, to ask, to listen, to sniff, to think, to write.

Aha. Where was I going to stay?

I didn't know.

So he would show me a good hotel. Maybe not that good, but good. The property of a friend, a once-great man. He would take me there and introduce me. And in fact Nadir Khouri took me straight from the airport to the Hotel Metropol and placed me under the protection of Habib Zacca.

In those days, the 1960s, the world was very interested in Africa. Africa was a puzzle, a mystery. Nobody knew what would happen when 300 million people stood up and demanded the right to be heard. States began to be established there, and the states bought armaments, and there was speculation in foreign newspapers that Africa might set out to conquer Europe. Today it is impossible to contemplate such a prospect, but at that time, it was a concern, an anxiety. It was serious. People wanted to know what was happening on the continent: where was it headed, what were its intentions?

The so-called exotic has never fascinated me, even though I came to spend more than a dozen years in a world that is exotic by definition. I did not write about hunting crocodiles or head-hunters, although I admit they are interesting subjects. I discovered instead a different reality, one that attracted me more than expeditions to the villages of witch doctors or wild animal reserves. A new Africa was being born—and this was not a figure of speech or a platitude from an editorial. The hour of its birth was sometimes dramatic and painful, sometimes enjoyable and jubilant; it was always different (from our point of view) from anything we had known, and it was exactly this difference that struck me as new, as the previously undescribed, as the exotic.

I thought the best way to write about this Africa was to write about the man who was its greatest figure, a politician, a visionary, a judge and a sorcerer—Kwame Nkrumah.

FROM THE STREETS OF HARLEM

In West End Square there is a human anthill.

A pyre has been erected; its flames shoot up. Who is going to be sacrificed?

Party cars with loudspeakers on their roofs have been driving around town all morning: 'All of you on the streets,' they broadcast, 'or at the market, or sitting at home or in your offices: COME AND EXPRESS YOUR ANGER!'

It does not have to be said twice. Declaring your feelings is a popular duty. And the population knows its duties. The square is full. The crowd is crushed together, but patient: it is hot, but it perseveres. Its thirst is agonizing, but there is no water. The sun is dazzling, but it is normal. It burns from below (the ground) and it burns from above (the sky) and, the best thing, gripped between these excruciating pincers, is to stand still: motion wears you out. With one fire below and one above, the crowd stands waiting for a third fire.

For the flaming pyre.

I ask here and there: What's going to happen? Nobody knows. They were told to come, and so they are here. They would not have been called out without a reason. And then, the surprised face of someone I've accosted: Why are you asking all these questions? Everything will be made clear. We'll know what's happening in due course. There's Welbeck now: Welbeck will tell us.

Minister of State Welbeck, stately and modest in a black Muslim skull cap, picks up the microphone. Hearing him is difficult, but you can pick up the sense: 'Imperialism is pushing . . . Nkrumah has been insulted . . . this slap in the face . . . we cannot . . . '

Ah, this is serious! Everyone strains to absorb Welbeck's message. Everyone nods their head—waves of nodding heads—and then grows still. The Minister continues: 'Imperialism would like . . . but we . . . and so never . . . '

'To the flames!' demand the impatient ones among the crowd, who are then hushed by their neighbours. Confusion, the commotion ebbs, stillness.

'The American weekly *Time*,' Welbeck continues, 'has written slanders about Nkrumah. *Time* has presented the leader, the creator and the magician of contemporary nationalism as a petty careerist.'

So, everything has been made clear. There is this weekly magazine called *Time*, and the Imperialists are insulting Kwame in it.

Here is the note that *Time* published on 21 December, 1959:

At first his people called him 'Show-boy.' Then he became his government's Prime Minister. This year he became his Queen's Privy Councillor. His local admirers now also refer to him as First Citizen of the African Continent. But when it comes to titles, there seems to be no stopping Kwame Nkrumah, 50. Last week the Accra *Evening News*, one of the Premier's more effusive admirers (it prints one or more pictures of him almost every day), announced that next March the people of Ghana would get a chance to decide two questions: 1) whether their country should be a 'full-fledged republic' no longer recognizing Elizabeth II as Queen of Ghana, 2) whether they approve of Nkrumah as first President for seven years. To the *Evening News*, there was only one man fit for the job. The man who is: Osagyefo (Great Man), Katamanto (Man Whose Word Is Irrevocable), Oyeadieyie (Man of Deeds), Kukuduruni (Man of Courage), Nufenu (Strongest of All), Osudumgya (Fire Extinguisher), Kasapreko (Man

Whose Word Is Final), Kwame Nkrumah, Liberator and Founder of Ghana.

The scandal is obvious. 'There seems to be no limit to the invention of titles.' And why should that be a concern of the gentlemen from *Time*? I feel the mood of the crowd flowing into me. I push towards the rostrum. I want to hear better.

'Such ignoble intriguing is ineffectual. The fact that we have Kwame is a blessing for Ghana, as it was a blessing for America to have Lincoln, for Russia to have Lenin, for England to have Nelson. Nkrumah is the priceless jewel in the crown of world nationalism. He is the Messiah and the organizer, the friend of suffering humanity, who has achieved his eminence by following the path of pain, service and devotion.'

Welbeck put that beautifully, and the people applaud approvingly. He let those gentlemen from *Time* have it. There is nothing for them here. And as I stand there in the crowd, writing, suddenly I notice that I am not feeling quite as stifled as I did moments before; that a space has opened around me; that those closest to me are moving away. I look around, and their eyes are not friendly, their gaze is cold, and a quick chill comes over me, and then I understand. I am the only white there, and I am writing in a notebook. Well, I must be a journalist. I am wearing a plaid-patterned shirt, so I am not English, because the English do not wear plaid-patterned shirts. But if I am not English, what could I be? An American. An American journalist! Good God, how can I get out of here?

'Burn! Burn!' chant the activists pressing towards the pyre. Violent shouts, threats, snorts, the stamping of feet. Welbeck's calls cannot be heard, although at this moment Welbeck has given the signal: 'Burn!'

They take handfuls of magazines and light them. The smoke billows out, because there is not a breath of air, and everyone rushes towards the fire, wanting to see.

Welbeck calls: 'Don't push! It's dangerous!'

Nobody hears. Whoever has a piece of paper in his hand throws it on to the fire.

The pyre burns.

A fanfare sounds.

Charred shreds of pages float up into the air. People blow and the scraps of paper flutter in mid-air; they laugh as bits of paper settle upon their heads. They are joking, calm, in a good humour again. Children are dancing around the fire. Look: they'll be able to bake bananas in it.

Welbeck has disappeared into a black limousine. His car flits through the lanes of Accra and out on to spacious Independence Avenue. The Minister is being driven to Flag Staff House.

To Nkrumah.

The Premier listens to Welbeck's report of the rally. The Premier will laugh, because here laughter is the response to everything that turns out well. The rally was a test. They passed: the people revere their Kwame.

Kwame—he is family, a brother. That is how they talk about him. A woman shows me her baby.

'What's his name?' I ask.

Kwame Nkrumah. She is wearing a dress with a print of the Premier's countenance. Kwame on her chest, Kwame on her back.

Nkrumah jokes: 'I would really like to know how many Kwame Nkrumahs there are in our country. I am afraid that I shall be remembered as a very prolific father.'

He himself married only recently. He likes to stress that throughout his life he has avoided women, money and

26

compulsory religious obligations: 'I believe that these three concerns should play a very small role in a man's life, since as soon as one of them becomes dominant, a man becomes a slave and his character is broken. I fear that if I consented to a woman's playing a serious role in my life, I would gradually begin to lose sight of the goal that I am trying to reach.'

Kwame establishes his goal when only a boy: the liberation of Ghana. In order to achieve it, he first has to make something of himself: that is his first task. In Ghana, a colony, a black man has no chance at a career. Kwame decides to study in the USA. His father—a goldsmith in a small town—has no money for his son's education. But Kwame has already finished teachers' college and is an instructor at the Catholic mission school in Elmina. He teaches for five years, saving, going hungry, hoarding every penny. He lives in terrible conditions, but he is scraping together the money for a ticket.

In 1935, at the age of twenty-six he travels to the United States. He is accepted at Lincoln University. How does he feel in that country?

'I travelled by bus from Philadelphia to Washington. The bus stopped in Baltimore, for the passengers to refresh themselves. I was dying of thirst, so I walked into the station buffet and asked the white American waiter for a glass of water. He frowned and looked at me out of the corner of his eye: "You can drink there." And he pointed to the spittoon.'

He studies, works, becomes politically active, makes money: 'If I was not busy twenty-four hours a day, I was wasting time.'

So: there is the night-shift at the Sun Company, in the Chester shipyards. 'Regardless of the weather, I worked from midnight until eight in the morning. Sometimes the frost was so severe that my hands froze to the steel. I studied during the day.'

So: he works in a soap factory. 'In the factory yard stood a mountain of discarded, rotting guts and pieces of animal fat. Armed with a pitchfork, I had to load that stinking merchandise on to a wheelbarrow. It was hard to keep from vomiting.'

So: he goes to New York during the vacation. 'In Harlem a friend and I would buy fish wholesale and spend the rest of the day trying to sell them on the street-corner.'

So: he is a steward on the S.S. *Shawnee*, on the New York–Vera Cruz line. 'The boss told me that I would be scouring pots until the end of the cruise. Later I advanced to washing dishes.'

He has nowhere to live.

In Philadelphia he is chased out of the train station by the police—he and a friend had been looking for shelter there—and spends the night in a park. 'We found a bench and lay down, thinking that we would spend the rest of the night there until fate turned against us. We had just fallen asleep, when it started to rain.'

He studies, attends meetings, works at self-improvement: 'I became a thirty-second degree mason and remained one throughout my stay in the United States.'

He is politically involved: 'I began organizing the African Students' Association of America and Canada. I wrote a brochure, *Towards Colonial Freedom*.'

He becomes interested in scientific socialism, in the works of Marx and Lenin at the same time he is studying theology as well: 'I devoted free time to giving sermons in the Negro churches. I was invited to this or that church almost every Sunday to preach.'

When he leaves the USA in 1945, he has three years as a philosophy instructor at Lincoln University under his belt

(Greek and Negro History). 'I was named the most distinguished professor of the year.'

He travels to London: 'One pleasure was buying a copy of the *Daily Worker*, the one newspaper I really wanted to read, carrying it in the most ostentatious way, and watching how many pairs of eyes quickly fixed on me.'

To heat the headquarters of the Union of West African Students, of which he is vice-president, he collects lumps of coal as he walks the streets.

At the same time, he is writing a doctoral dissertation in philosophy—on logical positivism.

He formulates his famous doctrine of the peaceful boycott, a doctrine of African socialism, based on tactics of constructive action without resort to force.

Kwame returns to Ghana.

It is 1947.

There might be five people here who know him personally. Perhaps a dozen. Not more. But it is this small group of people who head the newly established United Convention of the Gold Coast, a liberation movement but a movement that is very broadly based, highly undefined and without a programme. The members of the group pass as a collection of thinkers. They need somebody to do the dirty work. They bring in Nkrumah to do it.

This work is everything he has. 'In those days all my possessions fit into a small suitcase.'

A year later, he takes part in peaceful demonstrations and marches towards the governor-general's residence, towards Christianborg palace. Second World War veterans join in with a petition demanding autonomy for the Gold Coast. The police fire a few shots, and two are killed. Today, beautiful flowers grow on this spot. They show me this place a hundred times: two people died here for the freedom of Ghana. I stand there and lower my head.

Kofi Baako, a government minister, asks: 'Did anyone die for the freedom of Poland?'

Riots, arson and looting begin in Accra. The leadership of the United Convention of The Gold Coast lands in jail. Nkrumah is transported to the north, to the savannah. 'I was placed in a small hut there and kept under police supervision day and night.'

They release him, and when he starts back to work he sees that he has nothing in common with the leaders.

They want to make deals with the English in government offices.

He also wants to make a deal with the English, but, when he is doing so, he states, there must be an angry crowd outside the window.

Those Oxford men want to travel the road of legality. But Kwame has read Lenin. Lenin guides him on to the streets: Look, he says, there is power.

Power? Kwame wonders.

Crowded streets, the shouts of hawkers, children sleeping in the shade of the doorways. On the corners stand gangs of teenagers looking for a fight. The Muslims lie dazed by the sun. Sinewy labourers moaning under the burden of their sacks.

'Here is power!' insists the Russian. When the white man speaks, you do not want to have to believe in his words. But Kwame is alone. The leaders have turned away from him. They want to send him back to England.

Kwame appeals to the street. To the market-women, the teenagers, the labourers. To peasants and bureaucrats. To youth, above all to youth. That is decisive.

The English waver.

Kwame calls for a general boycott.

The country's economy seizes up.

The arrests, the repression, the truncheons return.

Kwame goes to jail. Crowds gather in front of the prison, singing hymns and protest songs. One is titled 'Kwame Nkrumah's Body is Rotting in Prison', and it remains vivid in my memory.

English concessions: they permit general elections (the first in Africa). Ghana votes in February 1951. Nkrumah's party carries a dizzying victory winning thirty-four of the thirty-eight seats in parliament.

A foolish situation: the party wins the elections, while its leader's body is rotting in prison. The English have to release him. On the shoulders of the crowd, Kwame is borne out of his prison cell and into the Premier's chair. Along the way the crowd stops at the West End Square: 'Here we performed a traditional purification rite. A sheep was killed as an offering, and I had to step barefoot into the blood of the sacrifice seven times, which was to purge me of the defilement caused by my stay in prison.'

The doors of his home never close. People come for advice or for help. They bring greetings. More than once he has talked to a visitor standing outside the door as he had a bath. 'I slept four hours on average. They give me no peace, they permit me no rest. Because I am a robot that is wound up in the morning and requires neither sleep nor feeding.'

When the premier goes to the country he sleeps in a hut. Sometimes he talks in the street until late at night and stays in some chance lodging instead of returning home. This way he wins over everyone he meets. And thus he spends his time.

Six years later, on 6 March 1957, Ghana gains its independence. It is the first liberated country in black Africa.

The crowd stands in West End Square. The crowd stands in

the sun, under the white African sky. The crowd stands and waits for Nkrumah, a black, patient crowd, a sweating crowd. This square, this brown frying pan in the centre of Accra, is full to its edges. Late-comers are trying to squeeze in and it will not take much more before the fence bordering the square begins to splinter, toppling the children perched atop the slats like bananas. It is hot.

Such a rally could be held nearer the sea. There is a breeze there and the palms offer shade. But what good are a breeze and shade if the historical resonance is lost? And history teaches us that, in 1950, Kwame Nkrumah called a rally exactly here, in the West End Square. The people also came and stood then, and that heat stood above the ground; it was January, the torrid month, the month of drought. Then, Kwame Nkrumah spoke about freedom. Ghana must be independent, and independence is something that has to be fought for. But there are three roads. The road of revolution. This, the speaker rejected. The road of closed-door pacts. This, too, the speaker rejected. And then there is the fight for freedom by peaceful means. The battle-cry of that struggle was proclaimed then, right here in West End Square.

Now it is the anniversary of that day, almost a holiday; the Premier makes a speech and says what every leader all over the world loves to say: 'Our road was the right one.'

Twelve tall poles have been positioned round the square. On each one hang eight portraits of Nkrumah, ninety-six in all. Nylon ropes run between the poles, and from the ropes are draped nylon banners: on the banners the Heineken beer logo. It looks like a great ship. The ship will never sail. It is grounded on the sand-bar of the city, and the people are waiting for what comes next.

Ministers and leaders of the governing party appear, filing on to the tribune. They are dressed for the occasion in mufti. The crowd comes alive and applause can be heard. If someone in the crowd is an acquaintance or cousin of a minister, he bellows a greeting: 'Hello, Kofi!' (to the Minister of Education). 'Hello, Tawiah!' (to Tawiah Adamafio, the party Secretary General).

They reply with a gesture and settle into deep armchairs. A clergyman steps up to the microphone. I recognize him: Reverend Nimako, the head of the Methodist Church in Accra. The pastor brings his hands together and closes his eyes. The old loud-speakers hung around the square cut out and die, but the sense of his thanksgiving-beseeching prayer is clear. The pastor thanks God for having blessed the people of Ghana. For having kept Kwame Nkrumah in His care. For having listened to the requests that have ascended to heaven from this corner of the earth. And then he asks that God not falter in His benevolence and that the future of this country be, through the will of the Highest, shining and unmarred.

'Amen,' murmurs the crowd, and kids set off two small bombs in the streets.

The pastor yields the microphone to K. A. Gbedemah, the Minister of Finance. He says that we have to wait because the leader has not yet arrived, and so he will review the history of Ghana's struggle for independence. In the middle of his story, it is reported that Nkrumah is on his way. The crowd rocks back and forth, people crane their necks, and children climb on to the shoulders of their elders. Tawiah Adamafio raises himself from his armchair on the tribune and calls out: 'Comrades, when our beloved leader app-ears, I want all of you to greet him by waving your handkerchiefs high over your heads. Ooo, like this'—he demonstrates, and the crowd rehearses twice.

Kwame Nkrumah stands on the tribune.

He is wearing grey mufti, as he is portrayed in the

monument by the parliament building. He holds a magic wand, a stretched monkey skin that, according to belief, drives away all evil and unclean forces from its bearer.

The square explodes with noise. The handkerchiefs flap and people chant: '*Jah-hia! Jah-hia!*' which means they are enraptured. Babies, until that moment asleep in bundles on their mothers' backs, stir uneasily, but their cries cannot be heard in that din.

Nkrumah is followed on to the tribune, now packed with sitting children, by six policemen in motorcycle helmets. Two of them stand at the corners of the platform, and four stand in a row behind the Premier's chair. They remain still, feet astride and arms behind their backs, until the meeting ends.

Nkrumah sits down in an armchair behind a small table covered with the national flag, and the square suddenly falls silent. The oppressive heat continues; even cheering is enervating. Somebody intones one of the party songs, but before the others pick it up, a pair of sorcerers comes into view. One of them is Nai Wolomo, chief wizard of the Ga region, where Accra lies. I do not recognize the other. They begin a ritual dance. Executing charmed spirals, they bow low to Nkrumah. They cannot bend towards the Premier without thrusting-out their backsides, which amuses the people who cheer and cry again: '*Jah-hia! Jah-hia!*'

The sorcerers stop in exhaustion and draw out two bottles of schnapps, a spirit exported from Holland that tastes of moonshine spiked with perfume. Now, however, the schnapps is an enchanted drink, transformed into a holy beverage, and the wizards offer some to Nkrumah. The Premier stands and drinks from a small glass held by a wizard, to renewed applause from the people. Now the rest of the drink, following spells and secret gestures supposed to propitiate the bad god of the sea, is poured on to the heads of those standing closest, as Polish boys douse girls on Easter Monday.

Nkrumah's speech begins. (The following day, the text of the address appeared in the *Evening News* under the title 'A NEW BIBLE FOR AFRICA'.) Nkrumah stands before the microphone, looking around the square, and says: 'Merry Christmas and a Happy New Year!'

It is 8 January, and so the people burst out laughing. Nkrumah pulls a serious face, and the crowd falls silent in an instant. The people wait, staring at him. Now Nkrumah laughs, and everyone laughs with him. He becomes serious, and the faces of everyone there become serious immediately. He smiles and the crowd is grinning. He begins in Fanti, saying that it is a long time since their last meeting, but he can see that they are all looking well.

'That's thanks to you, Kwame!' answer voices.

He looks over his shoulder, a signal for Adamafio, the Secretary General of the party, to approach, dragging a high lectern. On the lectern are the pages of his speech. It is in English. The Premier addresses his audience: 'Comrades and gentlemen!' Nkrumah speaks in a clear, measured way. His gestures are spare but expressive. Even the English say they take pleasure in watching him speak. He is of average height, but handsome and well-built, with an intelligent face and a high forehead and a sad look in his eyes. Even when Nkrumah laughs, he still looks sad.

He recalls his two maxims: first achieve the political kingdom and then you will conquer all the rest; the independence of Ghana is only an empty phrase until it is accompanied by the complete liberation of the African continent.

Kwame said that one battle for Ghana has been won: the country is free. Now the second battle is underway, for 'economic construction and liberation.' This battle is much more difficult and complicated. It demands greater effort, sacrifice and discipline.

He then attacks his own supporters sharply, striking out at party bureaucracy, at careerists and dignitaries.

'I must firmly warn those who, appointed by the party to responsible and influential positions, grow forgetful and believe they are more important than the party itself. I must warn those who join the party thinking that they can exploit it to their own advantage, praising themselves at the cost of the party and the nation.'

Whew! Do they like that! The square bestows a great ovation on the speaker. The square shouts: '*Anko*, Kwame! *Anko, anko!*'

'More, Kwame, again, oh, again!'

Amid the cheers, calls and chants a boy in a shirt displaying both the party and national colours (red, white and green) jumps up in front of the tribune and does vertiginous back-flips. Three back-flips in one direction, turn, and three in the other. Nkrumah stops speaking and looks at this feat with some curiosity. Three back-flips and then three somersaults. He is a good acrobat, believe me. He finally grows tired and disappears into the crowd amid its cheering.

Now, Nkrumah moves on to his favourite subject: Africa.

During the speech, Secretary General Adamafio stands near Nkrumah. Adamafio removes the pages that have been read, perusing the ones the Premier is in the middle of delivering. When Nkrumah sees a passage that will merit applause, he raises his hand in a gesture that means: Watch! Here it comes! And as he finishes the last sentence and Adamafio's hand whips the page away, the crowd goes wild. When the response is convincingly enthusiastic, Adamafio rubs his hands together and winks to those near him.

Nkrumah attacks the colonialists: 'Their policy is to create African states that are frail and weak, even if independent. The enemies of African freedom believe that in this way they can use our states like marionettes to continue their imperialist control of Africa.'

The crowd is outraged. People shout: 'Down with them! Down with them. Lead us, Kwame!'

The speech lasts three quarters of an hour. The crowd stands listening and reacting to every word. When Nkrumah finishes with the cry 'Long live the unity and independence of Africa!' a jazz orchestra in a corner of the square erupts in resonant boogie-woogie. Those closest to the orchestra begin dancing. The boogie-woogie carries across the square, setting people's hips rocking reflexively. But then the orchestra plays more softly: Joe-Fio Myers, the trade union general secretary, has begun reading a declaration of loyalty and support that the working people have delivered into the hands of Kwame Nkrumah.

We pushed towards the exit. On the street, far from the square, we met Kodzo. Kodzo is a post-office worker and boxing fan. He is my friend.

'Why didn't you go?' I ask. 'It was interesting.'

'What did Kwame say about wages?'

'He didn't say anything,' I admit.

'You see? Why should I have gone?'

Plan for a Book that Could Have Started Right Here

1

I have come home from Africa: a jump from a tropical roasting-spit into a snowbank.

'You're so tanned. Have you been in Zakopane?'

Will the Polish imagination never stretch further than Plock, Siemiatycze, Rzeszów and Zakopane? I'm working on *Polityka*. My current editor-in-chief, Mieczyslaw F. Rakowski, sends me into the provinces—yes, I'm to go on living in the bush, but in our own, native Polish bush. Somewhere, perhaps in Olecko or Ornet, I read that a great, almost global, conflict has broken out in the Congo. It is the beginning of July 1960. The Congo—the most closed, unknown and inaccessible country of Africa—has gained its independence, and at once the army revolts, the settlers flee, the Belgian paratroopers arrive, the anarchy, the hysteria, the slaughter—it has all begun; the whole indescribable *mélange* is on the front pages of the papers. I buy a train ticket and return to Warsaw.

2

I ask Rakowski to send me to the Congo. I'm already caught up in it. I've already got the fever.

3

The trip turns out to be impossible. Everyone from the socialist countries is being thrown out of the Congo. On a

Polish passport there would be no way of getting there. As a consolation, the travel committee allots me some hard currency and a ticket for a trip to Nigeria. But what's Nigeria to me? Nothing's going on there (at the moment).

4

I walk around depressed and heart-broken. Suddenly a glimmer of hope—somebody claims that in Cairo there's a Czech journalist who wants to force his way into the Congo by the jungle route. Officially, I leave for Nigeria, but secretly have the airline ticket rewritten for Cairo and fly out of Warsaw. Only a few colleagues are in on my plan.

5

In Cairo I find the Czech, who is named Jarda Boucek. We sit in his apartment, which reminds me of a minor museum of Arabic art. Beyond the window roars the gigantic hot city, a stone oasis cut in half by the navy-blue Nile. Jarda wants to get to the Congo by way of Sudan, which means by air to Khartoum, and then by air to Juba, and in Juba we will have to buy a car, and everything that will happen after that is a big question mark. The goal of the expedition is Stanleyville, the capital of the eastern province of the Congo, in which the Lumumba government has taken refuge (Lumumba himself has already been arrested and his friend Antoine Gizenga is leading the government). I watch as Jarda's index finger journeys up the Nile, stops briefly for a little tourism (here there is nothing but crocodiles; here the jungle begins), turns to the south-west, and arrives on the banks of the Congo river where the name 'Stanleyville' appears beside a little circle with a dot in it. I tell Jarda that I want to take part in this expedition and that I even have official instructions to go to Stanleyville (which is a lie). He agrees, but warns me that I might pay for this journey with my life (which later turns out to be close to the truth). He shows me a copy of his will, which he has deposited with his embassy. I am to do the same.

6

After a thousand problems getting a Sudanese visa, I change my Warsaw–Cairo–Lagos ticket for a Warsaw–Khartoum–Juba ticket at the United Arab Airlines office and fly to the Sudan. Jarda stays behind in Cairo to wait for another Czech. They will catch up with me in Khartoum and we will fly on together. Khartoum is provincial and nightmarishly hot—I am dying of boredom and the heat.

7

Jarda arrives with his colleague, Duszan Prowaznik, another journalist. We wait a few days for the plane, and finally fly to the southern Sudan, to Juba—a small garrison-settlement in the midst of an incredible wasteland. Nobody wants to sell us a car, but in the end we find a daredevil (in Juba, too, the opinion prevails that anyone who travels to the Congo is as good as dead) who agrees, for a large sum of money, to drive us to the border, more than 200 kilometres away.

8

The next afternoon we reach the border, guarded by a half-naked policeman with a half-naked girl and a little boy. They don't give us any trouble and everything starts to look enjoyable and idyllic until, a dozen or so kilometres on, in the village of Aba, we are stopped by a patrol of Congolese *gendarmes*. I forgot to add that back in Cairo the minister of Lumumba's government, Pierre Mulele (later the leader of the Simba uprising, murdered) had written out a visa to the Congo for us—by hand, on an ordinary sheet of paper. But who cares about that visa? The name Mulele means nothing to the *gendarmes*. Their grim, closed faces, half-hidden in the depths of their helmets, are unfriendly. They order us to return to the Sudan. Go back, they say, because beyond here it's dangerous and the further you go the worse it gets. As if they were the sentries of a hell that began behind them. We can't go back to the Sudan, Jarda tells them, because we don't have return visas (which is true). The bargaining starts. For purposes of corrupting I have brought along several cartons of cigarettes, and the Czechs have a box of costume jewellery. We bribe the *gendarmes* with a few trinkets (beads, clip-on ear-rings), and they permit us to go on, appointing a sergeant named Seraphim to escort us. In Aba we also rent a car with a local driver. It is an old, enormous, entirely decrepit Ford. But old, enormous, entirely decrepit Fords are by nature unfailing and in them you can drive across the whole continent of Africa and a bit more.

9

At daybreak we start towards Stanleyville: a thousand kilometres of muddy dirt road, driving the whole time through a sombre green tunnel, in a stench of decomposing leaves, entangled branches and roots, because we are travelling deeper and deeper into the greatest jungle in Africa, into an eerie world of rotting, proliferating, monstrously exaggerated botany. We are driving through a tropical wilderness that fills you with awe and delight, and every so often we have to pull the Ford out of the rust-coloured clay or out of a bog overgrown with brownish-grey duckweed. Along the road we are stopped by *gendarmerie* patrols, drunk or hungry, indifferent or aggressive—the rebellious, undisciplined army that, gone wild, has taken over the country, robbing and raping. When stopped, we push our driver Seraphim out of the car and watch what happens. If he falls into an embrace with the *gendarmes* we breathe easy, because that means Seraphim has come across his tribal kinsmen. But if they start punching his head and then beat him with the butts of their rifles, our skin crawls, because the same thing—or worse, perhaps—awaits us. I do not know what made us want to keep going along that road (on which it was so easy to die)—was it stupidity and a lack of imagination, or passion and ambition, or mania and honour, or our folly and our belief that we were obliged now to do it even though we had imposed an obligation upon ourselves?—and as we drive on I feel that with each kilometre another barrier has come down behind us, another gate has been slammed shut, and turning back becomes more and more impossible. After two days we roll into Stanleyville.

LUMUMBA

That man was here yesterday. They came in a muddy car, four of them. The car stopped in front of the bar. That man went in to drink beer. The other three wandered into town. The bar was empty; that man sat alone drinking beer. The bartender put on a record. Bill Haley sang 'See you later, alligator.'

'We don't need that,' said the one at the table. The bartender took the record off. The other three came in. 'Ready?' the one who was drinking beer asked. They answered 'Ready,' and the four of them left. There were people standing in the square, watching the four approach: the tall, slender man in front and behind him the three stout ones, with long arms.

Two girls started nudging each other because they liked that thin one. The thin one smiled at them, then at everyone, and began speaking. We didn't know who he was. We usually knew everybody who came to speak, but we were seeing this one for the first time. Before, the white used to come. He would swab at his forehead with a handkerchief, muttering various things. The ones standing in the front had to listen carefully and then repeat what was said to the ones standing further away. In the muttering there was always something about taxes and public works. He was an administrator, so he couldn't talk about anything else. Sometimes Mami came, our king, the king of the Bangs. Mami had a lot of beads and bracelets that gave off a hollow sound. Mami didn't have any power but used to say that power would return to the Bangs. Then the Bangs would take revenge on the Angra, who had pushed all of them away from the banks of the fish-filled Aruwimi River. Mami would shake his fist, and you could hear that hollow jangling.

But this man spoke differently. He told us that our tribe was not alone. There was a whole family of tribes and that family was called *la nation congolaise*. All must be brothers; there lay strength. He spoke for a long time, until night fell and the darkness came. The darkness took away all the faces. You couldn't see anything except this man's words. Those words were bright. We could see them distinctly.

He asked, 'Any questions?'

Everybody was quiet.

The speeches used to end this way, and whoever asked a question was beaten up afterwards. So it was quiet. Finally somebody cried out, 'You! What's your name?'

'Me?' That man laughed. 'My name's Lumumba, Patrice Lumumba.'

There he was: tall, lithe, rubbing his forehead with long nervous fingers. He had a face that they find attractive here because it's dark, but the features were European. Patrice was strolling the streets of Leopoldville. He stopped, turned around and started walking again. He was alone, composing his great monologue in his mind.

We are sitting in the room one evening when Kambi comes in. The look on his face is one I would prefer not to see again.

In a hollow voice, he says, 'Patrice Lumumba is dead.'

I think: the floor is going to cave in and we will crash two storeys to the ground. I look at Kambi. He isn't crying; he isn't shaking his fist; he isn't cursing. He is standing there helplessly. That is a common sight in this country: standing there helplessly. Because you've become a minister and you don't know what to do. Because your party has been shattered, and you don't know how to put it back together. Because you are waiting for help, and help isn't coming.

Kambi sits down and begins repeating over and over, mechanically like a rosary: 'It was the Belgians, it was the Belgians, it was the Belgians . . .'

I listened for the sounds of the city. To hear if they have started shooting. If the revenge has begun. But Stanleyville is dark, dead and mute. Nobody is lighting fires under stakes. Nobody is unsheathing the knives.

'Kambi, did you ever see Lumumba?'

No. Kambi never saw him. But he can listen to him. He and his friend Ngoy bring in a tape recorder which they plug in and start playing.

It is a speech of Lumumba's in parliament.

Kambi turns up the volume. Patrice is in full swing. The windows are open, and his words spill out into the street. But the street is empty. Patrice is speaking to an empty street but he can't see that: he can't know that: there is only his voice.

Kambi listens to the tape constantly. Like music. He leans his forehead on his arm and closes his eyes. The tape turns slowly, making a slight rustling sound. Patrice is calm, begins without emotion, even drily. At first he informs, presenting the situation. He speaks clearly, with a strong accent, enunciating each syllable diligently, like an actor mindful of the cheap seats. Suddenly his voice soars, vibrates, becomes piercing, tense, almost hysterical. Patrice attacks the forces of intervention. You can hear a light pounding—he is pounding his hand against the lectern to reinforce that he knows he is right. The attack is violent, but brief.

The tape falls silent except for the wavy rhythm of the machine. Kambi, who has been holding his breath, now gasps for air.

Again Patrice. His voice quiet, slow, with pauses between

the words. A bitter tone, disillusioned, the words catching in his throat. He is speaking to a quarrelsome hall, like a Renaissance congress of nobles. In a moment they will be shouting.

They don't shout.

The hall falls quiet. Patrice has them in his hand again. He explains, persuades. His voice drops to a whisper. Kambi leans over the reels. He can hear the confidence of the leader. Whisper, whisper, the rustle of the tape and whisper. The sound of breathing. You cannot hear the hall. The hall is silent, the street empty, the Congo invisible. Lumumba is gone; the tape keeps running. Kambi is listening. The voice regains its tone, strength, energy. The agitator is standing on the platform now. His last chance: to convince them, to win them over, to sweep them away. He stakes everything on that last chance. The tape spins: a maddening invasion of words, *l'unité*, *l'unité*, a crush of arguments, stunning phrases, no turning back, we have to go there, there where our Uhuru is, our straight spine, hope, and the Congo, victory, *l'indépendence*.

Now the flame is burning.

The tape flies off the reel.

I have heard how Nasser speaks. How Nkrumah speaks. And Sekou Touré. And now Lumumba. It is worth seeing how Africa listens to them. You have to see the crowd on the way to a rally, festive, excited, with fever in their eyes. And you need strong nerves to endure the moment of ecstatic screaming that greets the appearance of one of these speakers. It's good to stand in the crowd. To applaud together with them, laugh and get angry. Then you can feel their patience and strength, their devotion and their power. A rally in Africa is always a people's holiday, joyous and full of dignity, like a harvest festival. The witch-doctors cast spells; the imams read the Koran; the orchestras play jazz. The wind snaps the colourful crêpe, women vendors sell rattles, and the great ones talk politics from the rostrum. Nasser speaks tough, forceful, always dynamically, impulsively, imperiously. Touré banters with the crowd, winning it over with his good cheer, his constant smile, his subtle nonchalance. Nkrumah is turgid, intent, with the manner retained from his days preaching in the American black churches. And then that crowd, carried away by the words of its leaders, throws itself in exultation under the wheels of Gamal's car, lifts Sekou's car off the ground, breaks ribs trying to touch Kwame's car.

Meteoric careers, great names. The awakened Africa needs great names. As symbols, as cement, as compensation. For centuries the history of the continent has been anonymous. In the course of 300 years traders shipped millions of slaves out of here. Who can name even one of the victims? For centuries they fought the white invasions. Who can name one of the warriors? Whose names recall the suffering of the black generations, whose names speak of the bravery of exterminated tribes? Asia had Confucius and Buddha, Europe Shakespeare and Napoleon. No name that the world would know emerges from the African past. More: no name that Africa itself would know.

And now almost every year of the great march of Africa, as if making up for the irreversible delay, new names are inscribed in history: 1956, Gamal Nasser; 1957, Kwame Nkrumah; 1958, Sekou Touré; 1960, Patrice Lumumba.

None of them has laboriously climbed the ladder of government promotions, pinching votes and bowing to patrons. A wave of liberation struggle has carried them to the top: they are the children of storms and pressure, born of the longings and desires not only of their own countries, but of the whole continent. Thus, each of them becomes a sort of pan-African leader. Each of them will long to make his capital the Mecca of Black Africa.

This quartet is never to meet: Lumumba will not make it. Everything in the biography of the man comes down to the formula: he will not make it. In the years when a Kasavubu or a Bolikango is painstakingly fitting his clientele together, Lumumba is nowhere to be seen because he is either too young or is sitting in prison. Those others are only thinking of their own backyards, anyway, while Lumumba is thinking of the whole Congo.

The Congo is an ocean; it is a gigantic fresco of contrasts. Small clusters of people live scattered across a great jungle and a vast savannah, often unacquainted, knowing little about each other. Six people per square kilometre. The Congo is as big as India. It took Gandhi twenty years to cover India. Lumumba tried to cover the Congo in half a year. Absolutely impossible.

And for the Congo, as for India, the only way is to cover the whole country. Call on every village, stop in every small town, and speak, speak, speak. People want to have a look at their leader; they want to hear him at least once. Because what if he's the leader of some bad cause, some godless affair? You have to see for yourself, let him speak, and then decide if he's a leader or not. In other countries leaders have the press, radio, film and television at their fingertips. They have personnel.

Lumumba had none of this. Everything was Belgian, and there was no personnel. And say he had a newspaper: how many people would have been able to read it? Say he had a radio station: how many houses had radios? He had to criss-cross the country. Like Mao, like Gandhi, like Nkrumah and like Castro. Old photographs show all of them in simple peasant attire. Mao tightening his belt around a padded coat, Mahatma's skinny legs sticking out of his *dhoti*, Kwame throwing an ornamented *kente* over his shoulder, and Fidel standing there in a threadbare partisan's shirt.

Lumumba is always studiously elegant. The glowing whiteness of his shirt, his starched collar, his cufflinks, the stylish knot of his tie, his glasses in expensive frames. This is not the popular touch. This is the *style évolu* of the would-be European. When Nkrumah travels to Europe he demonstratively puts his African costume on. When Lumumba travels to an African village he demonstratively puts on European dress. Perhaps this is not even a demonstration of anything. But it is read that way.

Anyway, he doesn't spend a lot of time in the villages. Patrice was not the peasant-leader. Or the working-class leader. He was a product of the city, and the African city is not as a rule an agglomeration of the proletariat, but of bureaucrats and *petits bourgeois*. Patrice sprang from the city, not from the village. Not from peasants, but from those who were peasants yesterday. There's the difference. A person coming straight from the jungle to the Boulevard Albert in Leo reels around like a drunk. The contrast is too great, the jump too violent. Back there, he lived quietly in his tribe, and everything was comprehensible. Whether he liked it or not, the tribal organization gave him one thing: a balanced life. He knew that if he found himself in situation X, he should resolve it by method Y. Such was the custom. But in the city a man found himself alone. In the city there are the boss, the landlord, the grocer. One pays you, and the others have to be paid. There are more of the latter and that's when the trouble starts. Nobody cares about anybody else. Work finishes and you have to go somewhere. People go to the bars.

To tell the truth, Lumumba's career begins in the bars. In the clay-hut districts of Leo you can find 500 of them. The

African bar has nothing in common with, for instance, the Bar Lowicki back home in Warsaw. In the Lowicki a guy stands in line, gets a shot of vodka, munches a pickle and disappears. If he wants another drink, he has to stand in line again. A crowd, haste: cultural life is out of the question.

My favourite bar in Africa is called Alex. Often the names are more suggestive: 'Why Not?' 'You'll Get Lost' or 'Only You'. Recently, more high-flown signs have been hung out, like 'Independence', 'Freedom' or 'The Struggle'. Alex is a small one-storey shack but decorated like an inn for a country wedding—gay and extravagant. It stands in the shade of the palms, among billboards advertising Coca-Cola, Martell and Shell. In the morning it's virtually empty, but in the evening it draws a swarm of people. They sit on tin chairs at tin tables and drink beer.

There has to be beer. A lot of bottles and a lot of glasses. The bottle caps ring against the floor. From these caps the black pussy-cats make belts, which they wrap around their hips. The pussy-cat walks and the caps rustle. This rustling is taken to be exciting. There has to be jazz. And raspy Armstrong. The records are so worn out that they no longer carry melody, only that rasping. But the bar dances. It makes no difference that everyone is sitting down. Look at their feet, their shoulders, their hands. You can talk, argue and flirt, do business, read the Bible or snooze. The body always dances. The belly undulates, the head sways, the whole bar sways until late at night.

This is a second home. In their own homes they cannot sit around because it's cramped, grey, poverty-stricken. The women are quarrelling, the kids are peeing in the corner, there are no bright crêpe dresses and Armstrong isn't singing. Home is constraint and the bar is freedom. A white informer will not go to a bar because a white person stands out. So you can talk about everything. The bar is always full of words. The bar deliberates, argues and pontificates. The bar will take up any subject, argue about it, dwell on it, try to get at the truth. Everybody will come around and put in their two cents' worth. The subject doesn't matter. The important thing is to participate. To speak up. An African bar is the Roman Forum, the main square in a medieval market town, Robespierre's Parisian wine cellar. Reputations, adulatory or annihilating, are born here. Here you are lifted on to a pedestal or tumbled with a crash to the pavement. If you delight the bar you will have a great career; if the bar laughs at you, you might as well go back to the jungle. In the fumes of foaming beer, in the pungent scent of the girls, in the incomprehensible roiling of the tom-toms, names, dates, opinions and judgements are exchanged. They weigh a problem, ponder it, bring forth the pros and cons. Someone is gesticulating, a woman is nursing a baby, laughter explodes around someone's table. Gossip, fever and crowding. Here they are settling the price for a night together, there they are putting together a revolutionary programme, at the next table somebody is recommending a good witch-doctor, and further on somebody is saying that there is going to be a strike. A bar like this is everything you could want: a club and a pawn shop, a boardwalk and a church porch, a theatre and a school, a dive and a rally, a bordello and a party cell.

You have to take account of the bars and Lumumba understood this perfectly. He also stops in for a beer. Patrice doesn't like to keep quiet. He feels that he has something to say and he wants to get it out. Patrice is an inspired speaker, a genius. He begins with casual conversations in the bar. Nobody knows him here: a strange face. He's not a Bangal or a Bakong. What's more, he doesn't back any of the tribes. There's only one Congo, this stranger says. The Congo is a great subject, you can talk about it endlessly without repeating yourself. Such things are good listening. And the bar starts to listen. For the first time the bar falls silent, hushes, settles down. It pricks up its ears, ruminates, compares viewpoints. Our country is enormous, Patrice explains. It is rich and beautiful. It could be a superpower if the Belgians would leave. How can we oppose the Belgians? With unity. The Bangals should stop letting snakes into the huts of the Bakongos. That only leads to quarrels and not to *Fraternité*. You don't have freedom and your women don't even have enough to buy a bunch of bananas. This isn't life.

Patrice speaks simply. You have to speak simply to these people. He knows them. He too came from the village, he knows these people without timetables, shaken and disoriented, off the tracks, looking for some sort of support in the incomprehensible new world of the city, looking for some oar to grab hold of, for a chance to catch their breath before plunging back into this whirl of faces, into the confusion of the market, into everyday drudgery. When you talk to these people you can see how everything in their heads is tangled up in the most fantastic way. Refrigerators and poisoned arrows, de Gaulle and Ferhat Abbas, fear of the witch-doctor and wonder at the Sputnik. When the Belgians sent their expeditionary force to the Congo, they ordered the infantrymen to change into paratroopers' uniforms. I kept wracking my brains—why were they all paratroopers? Then it dawned on me: because paratroopers are feared here. In Africa they fear anybody who drops out of the sky. If somebody drops from the sky, he's not just anybody. There's something in it, and it's better not to go too deeply into such things.

Patrice is a son of his people. He too can be naive and

mystical at times, he too has a predisposition to jump from one extreme to another, from explosions of happiness to mute despair. Lumumba is a fascinating character because he is extraordinarily complex. Nothing about the man submits to definition. Every formulation is too tight. Restless, a chaotic enthusiast, a sentimental poet, an ambitious politician, an animated soul, amazingly tough and submissive at the same time, confident until the very end that he is right, deaf to the words of others, enraptured—by his own splendid voice.

Lumumba enchants the bars. From the very moment he walks in. He conquers them totally. Patrice always speaks with conviction, and people want to be convinced. They want to discover some new faith, because the tribal faith has become shaky. We used to say, 'Comrade, don't just agitate among us, give us something we can feel.' Lumumba knows how to give the bars something they can feel. He teaches, demonstrates, proves. The people say yes and applaud. *Il a raison*, they shout—'*He's right!*' And today in the Congo, when his name is mentioned, they repeat the same thing with melancholy reflection: *Oui, il avait raison.* Yes, he was right.

The Party Chairmen

There were three of them. They always walked together, as three, and drove around together, as three, in a big, dusty Chevrolet. The car stopped in front of the hotel, the doors slammed, and we could hear three pairs of feet coming up the stairs. They knocked, entered our room and sat down in the armchairs. If three people go around together in Poland, you don't think anything of it. But in the Congo, three people can be a party.

Our first conversation. They introduced themselves: 'Socialists from Kasai.'

Nice to meet you.

After a few pleasantries one of them came right out with it: 'We need money.'

'What for?' asked Jarda Boucek, my Czech friend.

'We want socialism to triumph in Kasai. And for that, we must buy off the leaders of our province.'

They were young, and you must make allowances for youth. So Jarda said that socialism does not triumph by means of money. He added something about the masses. 'The masses first,' that's how Jarda put it.

The socialists sat there, downcast. For them, the masses were not so important. Had we ever seen the millions marching here? The millions are passive, directionless, diffuse. All the action takes place among the leaders. Five hundred names, maximum. And it's exactly those names that you have to buy. Once you've bought a few, you can go ahead and set up a government, and the ones who put up the money determine the kind of government it will be. That's how the governments of Chombego, Kalonji and Bolikango were started. There are many possibilities, many untapped reserves. I quickly calculated that I had 1,000 dollars left. I wondered if I could buy myself a republic.

One with a real army, a government and a national anthem. I might not get much of a republic for my money. A thousand dollars is not a great sum. I would not be in the same league as Washington or London or Brussels. No: I had to forget about it. So did my friends. But to keep the conversation going, Jarda asked them about their party.

They represented the Kasai Socialist Party. They had a programme: drive out the Kalonji, stop the tribal wars, support a united Congo. A worthy programme.

'Is your party big?' Jarda asked.

They handed us the membership roll. The letterhead on the sheet of paper read: Kasai Socialist Party. Below it, we saw three names with their functions: party chairman, general secretary, treasurer.

Is that all? someone asked, tactlessly.

Yes, that was all, if you did not count the dusty Chevrolet, the chairman's wife and their two little boys. Pierre Artique, an authority in these matters, had determined that there were about ninety Congolese parties. One hundred and twelve of them ran in the 1960 elections, and if somebody said there were 200, you should know enough not to argue. At home, people shake their heads when they see these figures: too many. But it's not.

European countries have also had as many as 200 political parties, perhaps more. The parties, however, had come into being over a long stretch of time. Something would spring up, fail to sustain itself and die off. Life, time and the conditions of a normal political life effected a process of natural selection. Dominant parties existed but so, too, did the smaller parties, even if less significant. Some rose, others sank. The misfortune of the Congo was that there was no time. What took three centuries in other countries has happened here in three years.

In 1958, clusters of parties started bursting forth. Often,

several a week. Some might ask: why so many at once? Wouldn't three be enough or five? Of course they would be enough, but not in the Congo. The Belgians kept the Congolese not only isolated from the world, but also from each other, ignorant of what was going on in their own country. The average resident of the second-largest town in the Congo had no idea of what was going on in the third-largest town. If he wanted to go there, he had no money to pay for the trip. The distance between two towns in the Congo can be like the distance between, say, Warsaw and Madrid.

So a Congo People's Party arose in Leo. At the same time, identical parties were formed in Kindu, in Boende and in Kenge. None of them knew a thing about the others. Then came the moment of national independence, when the parties were to unite. The chairmen of the People's Parties assembled from Leo, Kindu, Boende and Kenge. They said to each other: Let's unite into one party. But one party meant one chairman. Who's going to be the number one chairman? They all wanted the job! None of them backed down—Why should I be the one to give in? I'm as good as you are, so what right do you have to give me orders? We might have advised these chairmen to consult the opinion of their grass-roots supporters, but, then again, the grass-roots supporters in Kindu did not know the chairman from Boende, and the chairman from Boende had nothing to say to the grass-roots supporters in Kenge, because he had never even been in Kenge. So the grass-roots supporters did not matter in the least; what did was what went on behind the scenes. Behind the scenes they were all quarrelling—obstinate and ambitious. This was the moment to establish your career, get a jump on everyone else, advance at a dizzying speed. And they believed, each one, that they all had the same chance. There were no party regulars, eminent thinkers, experienced administrators or decorated generals: they were all from the same mission schools; today they were petty party bureaucrats. But tomorrow—*tomorrow*—any of them could have been party chairman!

THE OFFENSIVE

The army moved out at dusk. We heard the roar of the motors and then eight big trucks drove through the square. The soldiers stood leaning on the handrails, in helmets, with rifles slung across their backs. It's not the custom here for the army to sing. They drove in silence through the empty city, through streets depopulated by the rigours of the curfew. There were perhaps 300 of them. The trucks turned on to the road out of town, the roar of the motors could still be heard, and then everything disappeared into silence, into jungle, into the violent twilight.

I wanted badly to go with them. I wanted to see the war; it was the reason we had forced our way into the Congo in the first place. But in the Congo we had found no war, only a brawl, absurd quarrels and heavy-handed imperialistic intrigue. There was nothing for us to do here. There were days when we didn't set foot outside the hotel because there was nowhere to go. There was no reason to go anywhere. Everything seemed either too inconceivable or too obvious. Even conversations were senseless. The Mobutu backers always considered the Lumumba backers animals, and the Lumumba partisans always regarded the Mobutu supporters as scoundrels. How many times can you listen to the same accusations? The one with the most patience was Fedyashin. Fedyashin was always getting somebody to talk, and then he would come back to us with a revelation: 'You know, this young fellow says that they have a lot of followers in Kindu.' I don't know what was wrong with me, but the fact that they had so many followers in Kindu did not particularly interest me.

That's why I wanted to go with the army. The army, unlike the banal running off at the mouth over warm beer, was a concrete reality. The army was now beginning an

61

offensive. In the heart of the continent, 300 soldiers were going off to war. But I couldn't be among them. I had a wolf ticket. You get that ticket when you cross a certain parallel. When you reach a place where you find out that you have white skin. This is a discovery, a sensation, a shock. I had lived for twenty-five years without knowing about that skin. A hundred children play in the courtyard of the townhouse I live in back home, and not one of them has ever given his skin a thought. They only know that if it's dirty, that's bad. But if it's clean and white—that's good! Well, they've got it wrong. It's bad. Very bad. Because white skin is the wolf ticket.

Books about Africa used to get on my nerves: so much about black and white in them. This colour, that colour, and all the hues in between. When I finally went myself, I understood. Right away you find out what's assigned to you, which line you're supposed to stand in. Right away that skin starts itching. It either affronts or it elevates. You can't jump out of it, and it cramps your style. You can't exist normally. You will always be above, below, or off to the side. But never in your own place. I was once walking through the black quarter of Accra. I was with a black student, a girl. As we walked, the whole street jeered. They called us the worst names; the cursing and the rage followed her. It was too much to bear. 'I had five people and twenty blacks with me,' an Englishman told me. It's the ones like him that help build the myth. The total, absolute myth of the colour of skin, still alive and powerful.

People ask why the blacks beat the whites in the Congo. Why, indeed. Because the whites used to beat the blacks. It's a closed circle of revenge. What is there to explain? People give in to the psychosis and it deforms and kills them. In the jungles of the Eastern Province I found a

Polish *émigré*. For a hundred kilometres around he was the only white. He was gravely ill. Sitting hunched over, he repeated mechanically, 'I can't take it, I can't take it.' He had been raised in the colonial world: a black man would be walking along, and a white gentleman and his lady would be driving back from a party, and if the black didn't get out of the way, the car stopped, the gentleman would get out and hit the black in the face. If the black was walking too slowly—in the face. If he sat down—in the face. If he mumbled—in the face. If he drank—in the face. The blacks have strong teeth, but they can get tired of having to take it and having to take it, even on a tough jaw. The world has changed: now it is the white *émigré* who sits and trembles, because his fillings are not very strong.

The strong teeth were on the offensive, and the rotten teeth were hiding in the corners. I too would have gone to the front, but I had a wolf ticket. I thought of going and explaining: I'm from Poland. At the age of sixteen, I joined a youth organization. On the banners of that organization were written slogans about the brotherhood of the races and the common struggle against colonialism. I was an activist. I organized solidarity rallies with the people of Korea, Vietnam and Algeria, with all the peoples of the world. I stayed up all night painting banners more than once. You never even saw our banners—they were great, enormous; they really caught your eye. I have been with you wholeheartedly every moment of my life. I've always regarded colonialists as the lowest vermin. I'm with you and I'll prove it with deeds.

We set out to do just that. To go with the offensive. With relief we left our stuffy hotel rooms and started across the city. It was hot, awfully hot, but nothing could hold us back. The downtown ended and we entered one of the quarters. Beyond was the army camp and headquarters.

That was our destination. But we didn't reach it, because an officer suddenly stopped us. He looked at us threateningly and asked us something. We couldn't understand the language. The officer was slightly built—we could have taken care of him easily—but a crowd of onlookers appeared at once, surrounding us in a tight circle. This was no joke. The officer swore and pointed his finger at us, and we stood there helpless and mute because our language was incomprehensible in the officer's ears. He started asking more questions. And we couldn't do anything. The soldier was becoming furious. This is where we get it, I thought to myself. But what could we do? We stood and waited. A boy on a bicycle rode out of a side street. He stopped and pushed through toward us. He understood French; he could interpret. We told him that we were from Poland and Czechoslovakia. He translated this. The people in the crowd began looking at each other, searching for a sage who would know what those names meant. The officer didn't know them, which made him angrier than before. There were more shouts, and we stood there as meek as sheep. We wanted to say that we were full of feelings of friendship, that each of us stood in solidarity with the struggle of the people, that our desire to take part in the offensive was proof, but the officer was shouting and we couldn't get a word in. He must have been insisting that we were Belgians; I don't know what he was after. Finally Jarda found a way out. Jarda lived in Cairo, so he had a driver's licence printed in Arabic. He took out the licence, showed it to the officer as the crowd watched attentively, and said: 'It's from Nasser.'

The magic of this word serves all over Africa. 'Aha,' the boy translated for him: 'So you're from Nasser. What a shame, that so many people in this world look like Belgians.'

'It's not our fault,' I said in Polish, 'not our fault at all.'

The officer shook our hands, turned about-face and walked away. The crowd dispersed and we were left alone. We could have kept going, but somehow everything had lost its sparkle. In fact, we had no reason to feel resentful. In Poland, too, there are a lot of people who don't know that such countries as Gabon and Bechuanaland exist, even though they really do. I once leafed through a Belgian history book written for Congolese schools. It was written in such a way that you could think Belgium is the only country in the world. The only one.

We were back to sitting around in the hotel. Jarda listened to the radio. Duszan read a book. I practised shadow-boxing.

More of the Plan of a Book that Could Have Been Written

10

In this book that I haven't written for lack of time and sufficient will-power, I would like to include the story of the few hours that we lived through after the night when Stanleyville learned that Lumumba had been murdered, and that he had died in circumstances so bestial that they trampled all dignity. We were wakened by someone's piercing shout in the morning. We jumped out of bed—I was sleeping with Duszan in one room, and Jarda was next door—and dashed to the windows. In the street in front of our hotel (it was called the Résidence Equateur), *gendarmes* were beating a white man to within an inch of his life. Two of them had his arms twisted back in such a way that the man was forced to kneel and stick his head out, while the third was kicking him in the face with his boot. We heard shouts from the corridor as other *gendarmes* went from room to room dragging whites out into the street. It was obvious that the *gendarmes* had begun a morning of spontaneous revenge directed at the white colonists whom they blamed for the death of Lumumba. I looked at Duszan: he was standing there, pale, with fear in his eyes, and I think that I too must have been standing there, pale, with fear in my eyes. We listened to hear if the sound of clumping boots and banging rifle butts against doors was headed our way, and, nervously, hurriedly, we started getting dressed because it's bad to be wearing only pyjamas or a shirt in front of uniformed people—it puts you at a disadvantage right away. The one in the street was screaming more loudly and was bleeding profusely. In the meantime, more whites appeared, pushed out of the hotel by the *gendarmes*; I didn't even know where these people were coming from, since our hotel was usually empty.

11

For an instant we are saved by chance or, more exactly, by the fact that our rooms don't open on to the corridor but on to the terrace at the end of the building, and the *gendarmes* hadn't taken the trouble to poke into every corner. They threw neighbours, now also beaten up, on to a truck and drove off. Immediately it grew as quiet as a graveyard. Jarda, who had come into our room, was carrying his radio. The Stanleyville station was giving government communiqués appealing to all the whites still in the city to stay off the streets and not to appear in public because of the behaviour of isolated elements and certain military groups which the government 'is not able to control fully.' Since there was no sense in sitting around in the room, we went down to the lobby, thinking that somebody might tell us what was going on. We were not tourists, but correspondents who had to work, and the more dramatic the circumstance, the more we had to work. There was no one in the lobby. We sat in armchairs, around low tables, facing the door. It was hot and we were developing a thirst for beer even though beer was not to be dreamed of. In the last few days we had become thoroughly famished. Our daily nourishment consisted of one can of Dutch sausages for the three of us. There were five little sausages to a can. We ate one sausage each and then drew lots: the one with the short straw didn't get a second sausage. Aside from those two sausages (or that one) we didn't eat anything, and on top of that, our supplies of sausages were running out. So we sat in the armchairs, thirsty and dripping sweat. Suddenly a jeep drove up in front of the hotel and a gang of young people jumped out with automatic rifles in their hands. It was clearly a hit squad, a vengeance patrol. Yes, you had only to look at their faces: they were out for blood. They came storming into the lobby and surrounded us, pointing their weapons at our heads. At that moment I honestly thought: this is the end. I didn't move. I sat immobile not because of any courage, but for purely technical reasons: it felt as if my body had turned to lead, that it was too heavy for me to budge it. Just then, when our fate seemed already to be determined, the following occurred: the leader of the squad trotted into the lobby. He was young, a boy, mulatto, with a mad look in his eyes. He rushed in, saw us and stopped. He stopped because he spotted Jarda. Their eyes met and they looked at each other in silence, without a word, without a gesture. They looked at each other in this way for a long while and the mulatto seemed to calm down, as though thinking something over. Then, without a word, he motioned to his people with his automatic rifle and they—also without a word—turned away from us, got back into the jeep and drove away.

'That's Bernard Salmon,' said Jarda. 'He was once in Cairo as Lumumba's envoy. I interviewed him.'

12

We went back upstairs to our rooms to write our dispatches about Lumumba's death and about what the city looked like afterwards—the city where he once lived and worked. Each of us wrote something brief because, as a matter of fact, we had little information and what we had lived through that morning was not fit to appear as part of the next day's official press coverage. There then arose the problem of taking our dispatches to the post office at the other end of town: we—that is, white people—would have to drive across a city terrorized by the *gendarmes* and the vengeance squads. I haven't mentioned that immediately upon arriving in Stanleyville we had pooled our resources to buy a very used car, a Taunus, from an Indian. In this car (Jarda was driving) we set off for the post office. A very hot and humid afternoon. The city was so deserted that we did not see a single car or person. It was the model empty city, dead concrete, glass, asphalt. Dead palm trees. We reached the post office building, alone in an open space. It was locked. We started banging on the doors, one after another. No one answered. Duszan found a small metal shutter that opened on to the cellar below, and we slipped into the dark, musty passageway. At the end there were stairs that led up into the cavernously empty main hall, covered with litter. We didn't know what to do next, so we simply stood there. At the other end of the hall was a door, and behind it were more stairs, leading to the second floor, and we went up to see if anyone was there. We started up to the third floor, the top one. If the police caught us in this place, deserted now but still strategically important, they would, we feared, treat us as dangerous saboteurs. Finally, going from room to room, we stumbled upon a hall with more than a dozen telex machines and a battery of transmitters. A hunched-over, dried-up African approached us from the corner.

'Brother,' I said, 'connect us with Europe. Connect us with the world. We have to send important dispatches.' He took our texts and sat down at the machine. We returned to the car; the street was empty. We were on our way back to the hotel and it seemed that everything would go well when suddenly a jeep full of *gendarmes* pulled out from around a corner and we found ourselves facing each other,

70

eye to eye. I don't know what happened, or rather, I think that what happened was this: the presence of whites in the street was so improbable that the *gendarmes* took our car for a phantom, an illusion—they were dumbfounded and they did not react. The confrontation lasted only a moment, because Jarda had the presence of mind to whip the steering wheel around and cut into the nearest sidestreet. We made a run for it. We hadn't reached the hotel yet when Jarda slammed on the brakes and brought the car to a stop in the middle of the street. We jumped out, leaving the doors open behind us, and sprinted for the hotel. When we locked the door of the room behind us, we were all panting and we wiped the sweat from our foreheads.

13

There were also calm, peaceful days, when we believed that we could appear in the streets without being beaten up and set out into town without fear. We might go to the airport, looking for our airplanes that were supposed to bring help. At that time the Gizenga government, or rather the handful of people who had managed to get from Leopoldville to Stanleyville with Gizenga, was officially recognized by our countries as the legal government of the Congo. We, in turn, were the only people who had managed to come to Stanleyville from Europe and the local authorities—having no one else at hand—treated us more like ambassadors and ministers than simple correspondents, drudges of the pen. The government, however, did not have full control of the situation and our positions were not esteemed enough to protect us against the fists of the angry populace. There was a small consolation in the fact that the authentic ministers of the Congolese government were beaten up by their own *gendarmes*, which we saw with our own eyes. And so, when a peaceful day came along, we repaired to the airport. We had found a spot on the porch of an abandoned house with a good view of the runway and we always went there. 'Today they'll come for sure,' Jarda would say each time. We would sit staring for hours into the sunny sky in which an airplane was supposed to appear. But nothing moved in the sky; and there was silence in the air. I doubted more and more that an airplane would ever come, but I never said so aloud, suspecting that Jarda might have had some special information after all.

14

One day a patrol of *gendarmes* appeared at the hotel. They took us to headquarters, the army command post, located on the grounds of the barracks. *Gendarmes* with their women and children wandered between the barrack buildings; they were cooking, washing, eating, lying around—it looked like a big gypsy camp. Sabo, a massive, reddish ogre, greeted us in the command post. He ordered us to sit down and then asked, 'When is the aid going to come?' I waited to see what Jarda would say because I thought he might know. Jarda told a story, that the airplanes were waiting in Cairo but had been refused the right to fly over the Sudan by its dictator and there was no other air route.

'We have nothing left here,' said the major. 'We have no ammunition, no food. The commander of the army'—that was General Lundula—'is himself distributing the last drops of gasoline. If nothing changes, Kobutu and his mercenaries will have us by the throat.' And here the major quite literally grabbed himself by the throat, so that the veins on his temples stood out. The atmosphere was tense and unpleasant; we felt helpless, weak. 'The army is rebelling,' the major went on. 'They are hungry and riled up; they refuse to obey orders, they are asking whose fault it is that no aid has come. If the aid does not arrive, the general staff will be forced to hand you over to the *gendarmes* as the culprits. That will calm things down for a while. I'm sorry, but I have no other way out. We've lost control of them'—and with his hand he motioned towards the window, through which we could see half-naked *gendarmes* wandering about.

15

We returned to the hotel: the first Christians, about to be thrown to the lions. To me it was obvious that help would never come, and Jarda and Duszan were now starting to share my fatalism. We had only a few days left to live. We tried feverishly to figure out what to do. We had to escape. But how? Escape was impossible. There were no airplanes and our car would be stopped on the way out of town. We wondered whether we should hide out in one of the houses abandoned by the Belgians. But that would give us only a few days, and somebody was bound to spot us and denounce us or else we would die of hunger. There was no way out: we were trapped, and the more we struggled, the more the noose would tighten. One hope remained: that I could talk to H.B., who could help us. H.B. worked in the United Nations headquarters in Stanleyville. People from the United Nations form a club unto themselves. Many of them are pretentious: they look on everything and everyone from a global perspective, which means, simply, that they look down. They repeat the word 'global' in every sentence, which makes it difficult to settle everyday human problems with them. Nevertheless, we decided that we should go to see H.B., who was an acquaintance of mine. He invited me to supper, since the UN always has enough to eat. I could not remember the last time I had eaten supper; indeed, for a long time, I had not eaten anything at all. During that feast, UN soldiers in blue helmets watched over us. Their presence enabled me to experience a blessed moment of security that evening, two hours in which I knew that no one was going to beat me, lock me up, or put a pistol to my head.

'Commissioner,' I told H.B. as he lay back in a colonial armchair after supper, 'my friends and I must get out of here urgently. We'd be very grateful if you were able to arrange things for us.' But in reply H.B. lectured me on the neutrality of the UN, which cannot help anyone because so doing would immediately lay it open to charges of partiality. 'The United Nations can only observe,' he said. I got the idea that my request had sounded rather unimpressive, and that I would have to bring up heavier artillery. At the same time, I could not let H.B. in on our reasons for having to clear out (and fast), because if he found out about our conflict with the Lumumbists he would immediately broadcast it to the whole world (that is, broadcast it globally).

'Commissioner,' I began in a new style, 'I wish you a long life and we know that, unfortunately, life is full of changes and one day you might be on top and the next day you might be on the bottom. There might come a day when you need my help'—I didn't believe it for a second—'so let's build a bridge. I will be the first to use it by crossing this raging torrent, but in the future, perhaps, this same bridge will allow you to cross a raging torrent of your own.' And H.B. helped.

16

Two days later a car flying the banner of the United Nations carried us to the airport. We had left our Taunus in the street, with the keys in the ignition. On the runway stood a four-engined aircraft without any insignia or markings. We had no idea where it might take us, but the important thing was to get out of Stanleyville. The people at the airport were saying that we would be flying to Juba (which meant to the north-east), but after take-off the aircraft headed south-east and an hour later we found that we were looking not at the monotonous brown-grey of the savannah but at the intense green of the Kivu mountains, awesome and soothing at once. This was Africa the arch-beautiful, the fairy-tale Africa of forests and lakes, of a cloudless and peaceful sky. The change in direction was puzzling, but there was no one to ask about it: the crew was locked in the cockpit, and we were alone in the empty fuselage of the aircraft. Finally the transport began its descent, and a lake as big as a sea appeared, and, then, beside the lake, an airport. We rolled towards a building with a sign that said 'Usumbura' (now Bujumbura, the present-day capital of the republic of Burundi, then a Belgian territory).

17

Le Monde, among other papers, later wrote about what was done to us in Usumbura. Belgian paratroopers were waiting on the airport tarmac. If they are soldiers from Belgium, I thought, they will treat us with humanity. But the units stationed in Usumbura were made up of Congo colonials—rapacious, brutal and primitive. They treated us not as journalists but as agents of Lumumba; they were elated that we had fallen into their hands. 'Passports and visas!' a non-commissioned officer said sharply. Of course, we had no visas. 'Aha, so you have no visas!' he rejoiced. 'Now you'll see . . .' They dumped all our baggage on to the ground and emptied out the entire pathetic contents of our suitcases. What does a reporter carry around the world? Some dirty shirts and a few newspaper clippings, a tooth-brush and a typewriter. Then the body search began, with their fingering every fold and seam, our cuffs, our collars, our belts and our shoe soles—all the while pushing, pulling, prodding and provoking. They confiscated everything—including our documents and money—and returned only our shirts, trousers and shoes. The terminal had a central section and two wings, and we were led to a room at the end of one wing and locked up. It was on the ground floor. A paratrooper was put on watch under the window. In normal times our cell must have served as a storage room for chairs—in it there were metal chairs which are, I've concluded, the most dangerous piece of furniture to sleep on, since, with any movement during sleep, the chairs slide away from each other and you fall to the floor (concrete), incurring varied and painful injuries to the body. The advantage of the chairs over the floor, however, consisted in the fact that the chairs were warm and not constantly damp. Being locked up is a wholly unpleasant experience—particularly at first, during that transition from a free to a captive state, that moment of the echo of the closing door. Many things go through your mind. For example, after a few hours I had begun to consider the question: is it better to be in jail at home or abroad? The immediate answer should be: wherever you are beaten less. But, if you put aside the issue of being beaten, it is, I concluded, better to be locked up at home. There, you can be visited by your relatives, you can write letters, receive packages and hope for amnesty. Nothing of the kind awaited us in Usumbura. We were cut off from the world. The paratroopers could do whatever they wanted with complete impunity: they could murder us, and nobody would be able to find out where or how we had been killed. We would simply have disappeared from Stanleyville.

We were interrogated. The interrogation was conducted by civilians, perhaps colonials from Stanleyville as they appeared to know the city intimately. They did not believe we were journalists. Of course. Nowhere in the world do the police believe that such a profession actually exists, often with some justice given the people who have become foreign correspondents. But we had little to tell them and finally they stopped tormenting us. The guards' shifts changed at nine in the morning and nine in the evening, and the paratrooper on night watch brought us our meal. That was when we were fed, in the evening, once a day—one bottle of beer for the three of us and a small hunk of meat each. The paratrooper who arrived in the morning began the day by leading us outside to the toilet, one by one: there was no bucket in our room; for sudden emergencies we needed special permission, which was granted grudgingly. They did not allow us to wash—in tropical conditions, a form of torture: the sweaty skin quickly begins to itch and hurt. Jarda's asthma then started up again. He had trouble breathing, and was choking from coughing fits. There was no doctor. From our window we had a view of the following: first, the helmet and shoulder of the paratrooper; then the flat ground that led down to the lake; and in the far distance the mountains ringing the horizon. From time to time airplanes landed and took off and we watched them. The days flowed by, one after the other, wearisome, monotonous, uneventful. The paratroopers said nothing. Not a single representative of any higher authority appeared. Then one evening a new paratrooper took the watch. He spoke to us; he was trying to sell us hippopotamus teeth. We had no money—it had been taken from us during the search—but we promised that, if set free, we would buy teeth, when our money was returned. He would end up helping us a great deal. It was a different paratrooper standing guard when an African approached our window the next afternoon, a tall, portly Tutsi with a serious, intelligent face, who said quickly, before he was chased away, that he had overheard officers in the airport coffee shop saying that we were to be shot the next day. The guard came trotting over and the man disappeared.

18

What I am writing is not a book, but only the plan (and a plan is even less substantial than an outline or a sketch) of a non-existent book, so there is not enough space to describe what really goes through the mind of a person who has just heard repeated the conversation of officers in the airport coffee shop from a tall, serious Tutsi. The almost instantaneous symptoms, however, are these: a state of depressing emptiness, collapse, dulled inertia, as if he has found that he is suddenly under the influence of a narcotic, or an anaesthetic, a strong dose of some stupefying medicine. The condition worsens: he starts to feel utterly powerless and to realize, fully, that there is nothing he can do to change or influence his circumstances. All the strength suddenly empties out of his muscles, leaving him too little energy even to scream, slam his fist against the wall or beat his head on the floor. No, it is not his body any more; it is foreign matter that he has to drag around until someone frees him of the enervating burden. It becomes stuffy, and you feel the stuffiness intensely—somehow, the stuffiness becomes the most palpable thing you know. Duszan and I sat there, not looking at each other: I can't explain why. Jarda lay across the chairs, sweating, tormented by his asthma attacks.

19

A sleepless night.

20

The rain began falling during the night. At first light the rain was still falling; it was cloudy and damp and fog lay on the lake. At dawn an airplane emerged from out of the mist and parked on the side runway, not far from us. This was unusual: every other airplane (the few that had landed here) parked on the other side of the airport, far away; but this one—perhaps because of the poor landing conditions?—was sitting right there on our side, where there was less fog (this part was the farthest from the lake). Two white pilots got out and went straight to the main terminal, but a few black stewards remained behind, hanging around the airplane. We called out to them, waving our hands. The honest paratrooper with the hippopotamus teeth had taken the night watch—our man, a man who just wanted to make a little money and survive, in other words an ordinary man (I became convinced that the ones who want to pick up a few pennies are often more human than the formal, incorruptible ones)—and when he saw that we wanted to talk with the stewards he moved around to the other side of the building. A steward came over, and Jarda asked him where they were flying to.

Leopoldville, he replied.

Jarda told him briefly about our situation, that our hours were numbered, and then begged the steward (a white begging a black) to go to the local United Nations headquarters as soon as he arrived in Leopoldville and tell the people there that we were in prison, that they should inform the world about us because then the paratroopers would not dare kill us and that they should send the army to rescue us.

Looking at us, the black man would have seen the frame of the window, and in that frame he would have seen bars, and behind those bars three white faces, horribly dirty, unshaven, exhausted: Jarda's face, round and full, and Duszan's and mine, thin. 'OK,' he said. 'I'll see what I can do.'

21

The hours of torture began. The steward had tossed a crumb of hope into our cell and it jolted us out of our state of paralysis and overpowering depression, a kind of self-deafening that I now see was a defence against insanity. For those awaiting death as we were, passive and apathetic, on the verge of collapse, ready to hit bottom, it takes only one flash of light in the darkness, one lucky break, and suddenly you rise up again and return to the living. What you leave behind, however, is an empty territory that you cannot even describe: it has no points of reference or shape or signposts, and its existence—like the sound barrier—is something you feel only once you have approached it. One step out of that emptiness and it disappears. No one, however, who has entered this emptiness can ever be the same person he was before. Something remains—a psychological scar, hardened, gangrened flesh—a fact, finally more apparent to others than to himself, that something has burned out, that something is missing. You pay for every meeting with death.

We watched the airplane take off and then began pacing feverishly among the chairs, talking and arguing, although, for all of the previous afternoon and evening and night, the cell had been silent. Would the steward really inform the United Nations? And if he did, who would he talk to? To someone who will take him seriously? To someone who will wave his arms around and do nothing? And even if he is taken seriously, will anyone be able to free us? And if everything worked in our favour, it would take at least half a day for the steward to fly to Leopoldville and talk with headquarters, and then for Leopoldville to notify the Usumbura headquarters. Before anything happened, the paratroopers could take us out and finish us off a hundred times or turn us over to Muller's hirelings. Thus came the nerves, the war of nerves, fever and agitation, but all of it inside, in us, because outside beyond the window it was always the same: the helmet and shoulder of the paratrooper and, further off, the plain, the lake (Tanganyika), the mountains. And today, in addition, the rain.

22

In the afternoon we heard a car motor under the window, and a screech of brakes, and then voices speaking in a language I did not recognize. We clung to the bars. Near the building stood a jeep flying the United Nations flag; four black soldiers in blue helmets climbed out. They were Ethiopians from the Imperial Guard of Haile Selassie, who formed part of the United Nations military contingent in the Congo. They posted their own guard alongside the paratrooper.

23

I have no idea what the Congolese who saved our lives was called. I never saw him again. He was a human being: that's all I know about him.

24

And not only do I also not know the name of whoever it was at the UN headquarters in Leopoldville who saved our lives, but I never even saw him. There is so much crap in this world, and then, suddenly, there is honesty and humanity.

25

I can't say if there was actually any bartering between the Ethiopians and the paratroopers over our fates. I can say that they didn't like each other, and they treated each other spitefully. They were competing for the prestige of controlling the Congo.

26

The next morning we took a Sabair flight out through Fort Lamy and on to Malta and then to Rome. In the great glass block of Fumicino airport, we watched the splendid and—to us, at that moment—exotic world of contented, calm, satiated Europeans on parade: fashionably dressed girls, elegant men on their way to international conferences, excited tourists who had flown in to see the Forum, meticulously preserved women, newlyweds flying off to the beaches of Majorca and Las Palmas; and, as the members of this unimaginable world passed by us (we were a disreputable-looking trio, three dirty, smelly, unshaven men in horrible shirts and homespun trousers on a chilly spring day when everyone else was in jackets, sweaters and warm clothing), I suddenly felt—the thought horrified me—that, sad truth or grotesque paradox that it might be, I had been more at home back there in Stanleyville or in Usumbura than here now.

27

Or perhaps I simply felt lonely.

28

The police looked us over suspiciously and I couldn't blame them. We could not go into the city because we had no visas. The police phoned our embassies, which had been looking for us all over the world. The ambassadors came out to the airport, but it was already late in the evening and we had to sleep there because we would not have visas arranged for us until the next day.

29

I returned to Warsaw. I had to prepare a note on what I had seen in the Congo. I described the battles, the collapse, the defeat. Then I was summoned by a certain comrade from the Ministry of Foreign Affairs. 'What have you been writing, you?' he stormed at me. 'You call the revolution anarchy! You think that Gizenga is on the way out and Kobutu is winning! These are pernicious theories!'

'Go there yourself,' I answered in a tired voice, because I still felt Stanleyville and Usumbura in my bones. 'Go ahead and see for yourself. And I hope you make it back alive.'

'It's regrettable,' this comrade said, concluding our discussion, 'but you can't return overseas as a correspondent because you do not understand the Marxist-Leninist processes that are at work in the world.'

'OK,' I agreed. 'I've got some things to write about here, too.'

30

I went back to work at *Polityka*, travelling around the country, writing up what I saw. In the Congo things turned out the way they had to, which in the end had been obvious to everyone who was there. A few months later I received an offer to travel to Africa for several years. I was to be the first Polish correspondent in black Africa and was to open a bureau office for PAP, the Polish Press Agency. At the beginning of 1962 I was sent to Dar es Salaam.

MARRIAGE AND FREEDOM

What follows is the complete and exact text of a letter sent to me by Millinga Millinga, an activist in the *Frente de Libertaçao de Moçambique*, the Mozambique Liberation Front. Millinga Millinga is a close friend: influential, serious, a figure at political rallies and diplomatic receptions.

L. Millinga Millinga
P.O. Box 20197
Dar es Salaam
Tanganyika

Dear Friend,

PERSONAL MATTER

At this critical moment in my life, compelled by an immense and unsolvable DILEMMA, I feel no shame in revealing deeply concealed problems that I have incurred in the preparation of my future, nor do I feel any shame in revealing them to you especially, a friend whose kindness and assistance have never been wanting on occasions of this kind in the past.

As you know, I am one of the Freedom Fighters who has devoted all his time to the struggle and receives no compensation. But in view of the fact that a human being cannot escape from his natural needs, I have for two years been plunged in heavenly love for Miss Veronica Njige (district secretary of TANU, the Tanganyika African National Union) of the Morogoro district, whom I have promised to marry. However, as I have been so deeply engaged in the struggle, and, moreover, given the particular circumstances in which FREEDOM FIGHTERS live, I have been unable to fill our treasure chest with funds sufficient for the preparation of a festive wedding. In addition, the parents of the Lady of my Heart are demanding fifty pounds as a dowry, plus, in lieu of cows and goats, another twenty-five pounds as a gift for the cousins. After calculating precisely all the necessary expenditures incurred from the preparations and the wedding day ceremony, the total sum of money required to meet my aims amounts to not less than 200 pounds, including the items mentioned above.

In the opinion of my Beloved the date for the wedding has been delayed too many times already and so she has taken to writing to me three times a week, demanding that a wedding be held before November 1962. In these letters there is nothing more than one simple and clear statement: 'FREEDOM AND MARRIAGE BEFORE NOVEMBER 1962.' Despite my relentless declarations on the theme of my present financial situation, with which she has no sympathy whatsoever, the Lady of my Heart insists resolutely on a wedding IMMEDIATELY because, a Freedom Fighter herself, she states categorically that she would prefer to suffer with me in our own home than remain in her parents' care. To a certain extent, I feel sorry for her. She is a grown woman, ready for marriage, and is always telling me, passionately, that she has, at present, strong desires, unprecedented desires, to become a wife without delay, and, acceding to her many requests, I have been compelled to agree that by 3 October I will pay her parents and relatives the seventy-five pounds and that the wedding will take place on 1 November 1962.

Dear friend, I would like you to turn over in your mind the true meaning of the sentence: 'LOVE IS THE

MISTRESS OF THE WISEST MEN AND THE MOTHER OF EVERYTHING.' If you think about this sentence in relation to the matters presented here, you will certainly adopt an attitude sympathetic to my present situation. Under these conditions I have nothing more to say, except to ask you to give me as much financial help as you can afford. I should stress here that this support is to be treated as private aid to me, MILLINGA, and not as aid to the Mozambique Liberation Party or to me in the role of its General Secretary. For this same reason, all payments should be addressed to my private post office box: Millinga Millinga, P.O. Box 20197, Dar es Salaam, Tanganyika. Payments sent in connection with the matter presented above will be confirmed by myself personally or by my cousin W. L. Mbunga, whom I have appointed to the post of Personal Secretary in Charge of Fundraising for my Wedding. His signature is to be found below.

In hopes of hearing from you before the deadline,
With fraternal greetings,

[Two illegible signatures]

I gave Millinga as much as I could afford, but it was obvious that some of the embassies must have given Millinga as much as he needed for the wedding took place (Millinga had mimeographed his letter and sent out many copies). I met both of them several days ago at a reception at the Soviet Embassy. Millinga, small, delicately built, permanently unshaven, stood silent and musing beside a stout, big-busted, gloomy girl, the Lady of his Heart.

THE CHILD-SUPPORT BILL IN THE TANGANYIKAN PARLIAMENT

The *Tanganyika Standard* of 21 December 1963 reported that 'the discussion over the child-support bill that erupted in the last session of parliament was the stormiest debate in the nearly two years' history of independent Tanganyika's Legislative Chamber.'

Delegate Lucy Lameck, the Vice-Minister of Co-operatives, an activist known for her emancipationist stance and a proponent of European examples and models of behaviour for African women, introduced the government-sponsored bill on child support (the Affiliation Ordinance Amendment Bill of 1963). She began by saying that in a country like Tanganyika, which has embarked on the path of modern development, 'newer and newer problems' will continue to arise. 'In earlier African society,' said the delegate, 'moral principles were not exposed to such great external pressures as today, and for this reason there was no need to create laws to protect the fate and upbringing of children born out of wedlock.' Now, however, it is imperative to find 'new remedies for the new problems affecting the population of urban centres.'

'The child-support bill,' Delegate Lameck stressed, 'arose as a result of research into the situation of African women in the cities. It turned out that, in Dar es Salaam, 155 out of 340 working girls had from one to six illegitimate children. The average monthly income of these single mothers was only 168 shillings a month, and no more than eight of them received any help from the fathers of their children.' The delegate also cited testimony from a school principal in Dar es Salaam, who stated that each month three or four girls dropped out of school as a result of pregnancy. This school taught girls between the ages of eleven and fifteen. The principal knew nothing about the ultimate fortunes of the drop-outs. 'In this situation,' concluded Delegate Lucy Lameck, 'it is necessary to introduce a statute requiring the payment of child-support by the fathers of illegitimate children.'

The debate that, as the *Tanganyika Standard* reporter wrote, 'destroyed the traditional seriousness of parliament' now began.

Delegate P. Mbogo (Mpanda) expressed the opinion that the child-support bill would lead to a widespread increase in prostitution. 'Girls are going to want to have as many illegitimate children as possible, because that way they will make money for cosmetics. Those girls will be like an underdeveloped country—they will have to be invested in.'

According to Delegate B. Akindu (Kigoma), the child-support bill would create 'a special danger for wealthy people, such as for instance delegates to parliament, because pregnant girls will be able to falsely proclaim that the fathers of these illegitimate children are government ministers or delegates to parliament . . . These perfidious beings,' the delegate said, 'will sow neo-colonialist propaganda in the hope of extorting money from rich men.' The delegate stated that many 'TD men' (the letters 'TD' appear on the license plates of cars belonging to high state officials) invite girls walking the streets into their cars. In such cases, it is up to the girl to refuse. 'If you cannot restrain your desires, find yourself a husband and do so quickly,' the delegate begged the girls of Tanganyika.

Delegate R. S. Wambura (Maswa) saw no need to introduce a child-support law since—in accordance with African tradition—legitimate and illegitimate children were treated the same way. 'This law,' the delegate stated, 'can only incite women to make money from their charms. And besides,' the delegate said, 'our girls usually have many men, which is going to make it hard to decide who the father is.' The speaker advanced another argument. 'This bill runs against the laws of nature, because it is known that the unemployed are equally capable of making babies, and yet the unemployed have no money for paying child support.'

Delegate R. S. Wambura enjoyed the support of Delegate Chief A. S. Fundikira (Tabora): 'The illegitimate child poses no problem in the African family; on the contrary, it is another pair of hands to work in the fields.'

The Minister of Justice, Delegate Sheik Armii Abedi, spoke in defence of the proposed government legislation. In the minister's words, 'If a man doesn't want it, he can proceed in such a way that the woman with whom he is dealing will not become pregnant.' The minister urged that the child-support law cover both working and unemployed men. 'If the law does not apply to those without money, the unemployed are going to feel that the government has given them full freedom to produce children by the dozen. The production of children—that will be the work of the unemployed,' stated the minister among applause and laughter from the delegates' benches.

Delegate F. Mfundo (Handeni) mentioned that the distinction between legitimate and illegitimate children was erected only under colonialism—traditional African law makes no distinction—and that therefore, a child-support law revealing a preference for illegitimate over legitimate children (the bill does not, after all, require the payment of support for legitimate children) was 'a reflection of the colonial mentality'.

Urging acceptance of the bill, Delegate Lady Chesman (Iringa) challenged Delegate Mfundo. Thanks to this legislation, she said, financial responsibility for illegitimate children would rest on the men, freeing the state of the obligation to build orphanages and allowing it to assign more funds for the struggle against Tanganyika's three principal foes: ignorance, poverty and disease.

The next speaker, Delegate A. S. Mtaki (Mpwapwa), stated in a lengthy presentation that the child-support law would have dreadful social consequences. First, it would cause a widespread increase in murder. 'People who are forced to pay support for illegitimate children are going to murder them—murder costs nothing.' Second, the rate of marital infidelity would rise: 'As a result of this legislation, men will avoid contact with unmarried women, and instead seduce the wives of others.' Third, the divorce rate would go up, 'because, as the married man would have to pay support for an illegitimate child, his wife was bound to discover what occurred and demand a divorce, or perhaps even leave him at once.' Summing up, Delegate Mtaki opined that 'experts in this field, such as Karl Marx, teach us that prostitution is capitalism.'

Victor Mkello (Dar es Salaam) vigorously supported Delegate Mtaki, demanding that the government withdraw 'this unfortunate legislation.' In the delegate's view, the law would force men to marry chance female acquaintances merely to avoid payment of child support. 'Such marriages will never be happy.' The government should take steps towards 'making girls aware of how to avoid pregnancy.'

The Vice-President of Tanganyika, Delegate R. Kawawa, argued on behalf of the government and denied that the proposed legislation would lead to a growth in prostitution, since the growth of prostitution is already restrained by other laws. The Vice-President also criticized the idea of teaching women how to avoid pregnancy. 'Such views are alien to our society and have been imported from outside,' the Vice-President said. 'Teaching women to avoid pregnancy would be nothing but an inducement for people to perform immoral acts.'

Delegate Bibi Mohammed (Rufiji), the director of the women's division of the governing TANU party, defended the bill. 'In some tribes,' she said, 'girls are locked up at home on attaining maturity, so that their parents can be sure they will not become pregnant. Yet men are like rats: they sneak into the house, and, as a result, the dumb-founded parents realize after a certain time that the girls, despite being kept under lock and key, are pregnant. Men never have enough: every one of them, even if he has conquered sixty women, will keep chasing and trying to get his hands on women whenever he has a chance.' Delegate Bibi came out strongly against the speakers who had objected to the bill: 'Delegates, as representatives of the entire Tanganyikan nation, ought to think about women as well as men, and they should not take advantage of the fact that they outnumber women in parliament to block legislation that would be of great benefit to women and men alike. Who of you, delegates, can say that he has a clean conscience? Many women come to me from all over and tell me that this or that delegate is the father of their child. I have promised these women that I will stand up in parliament and name names . . .'

At this point, Delegate Bibi's speech was interrupted by Delegate J. Namfua, the Vice-Minister for Trade and Industry, who said that Delegate Bibi should either restrain herself or stop speaking altogether. In his opinion, she has 'strayed too far from the issue at hand.' Delegate Bibi agreed that in fact 'it would be better for me to stop here, because I can see that too many delegates who are interested parties have very troubled expressions on their faces. I want to add one more thing,' Delegate Bibi concluded, 'which is that many girls die as the result of abortions. If we accept this legislation, nobody will need to have an abortion and we will save the lives of many young people.'

Delegate M. S. Madenge (Tabora) stated next that he would support the bill if it applied to schoolgirls, but if it was to be extended to girls from the street he would definitely oppose it.

A similar position was taken by Delegate H. S. Sarwatt (Mbulu) who took the position that the legislation would 'lead to a decline in morality among women.'

Another Delegate, M. S. Haule (Kondoa), pointed out that according to the last census, there were 5.5 million women and four million men in Tanganyika. 'This disproportion has arisen through the will of God,' stated the speaker, 'and we should draw the conclusion from this that God permits a man to have more than one woman. Therefore, this legislation intends to violate the natural order of things.'

The outcome of this debate was that ninety-five per cent of the Chamber came out strongly against the government child-support legislation. Although the Tanganyikan parliament consists exclusively of members of the ruling TANU party and had always given its unanimous approval of all bills placed before it by the Nyerere government, this was the first case in which virtually the entire Chamber had taken an anti-government stand. The government had to back down. Long procedural discussions between the government and parliament led to a compromise: a commission of five was established to make a fresh examination of the child-support bill.

ALGERIA HIDES ITS FACE

Ahmed Ben Bella, the president of Algeria, was overthrown on 16 June 1965. It happened during the night-time changing of the guard, just after two o'clock in the morning. Ben Bella lived on the Avenue Franklin Roosevelt, about half-way between the stifling, overcrowded centre of Algiers and the exclusive villa quarter known as Hydra. His house, though it bears the lovely name Villa Joly, was not particularly distinguished, just as the presidential offices were, while elegant, hardly grand. Those invited to Ben Bella's home remember that he would always have to open the gate himself with a key and, being absent-minded, was always having to look everywhere for it. Ben Bella was forty-six and lived alone.

Ben Bella was modest, uncommonly honest and scrupulous about material affairs. He drove a Peugeot 404, a car that in other African countries would be driven by no one more senior than a department head. This was not a calculated modesty. The president always had an inborn, natural disregard for worldly goods. He ate at odd hours, on the run, and his clothes could never have been described as fine. These were simply things he did not care about.

Although forty-six, Ben Bella seemed much more youthful—physically and mentally. He was, as we might say, an example of the *eternal youth*. When I saw Ben Bella in Addis Ababa in 1963, I would have said he was thirty-six, thirty-seven. He had thick black hair that grew low on his forehead and a strongly expressive face, a masculine face, young, with fair skin. I was always struck by the infantile aspect of that face, an aspect that suggested boyish caprice, whimsy. In fact, Ben Bella had an uneven nature. Everything about him was fluid, uncoordinated, contradictory. He was a seething element, electrified, one that

95

could not be confined. In an instant, Ben Bella might easily jump from one mood to another. He was impulsive, gusty, swept by passions. He would get impatient, and that impatience finished him. When excited, he would let words fly, unchecked, unconsidered, and then make irrational decisions that he would have to disown the next morning. 'Ben Bella put the leadership in a situation,' one of his close associates said later, 'where nobody knew what to hold on to.' His behaviour reflected the traits of his character. From prison he developed a peculiar habit of relaxation; he could sit for hours without moving, with his face of absolute stone, not a single muscle stirring. The effect was eerie. Suddenly, he would come to life, become ecstatic, gesticulate violently as he spoke, until, exhausted and smiling, he then calmed down again. The terrific stress of his life must have destroyed his internal harmony.

Ben Bella's character riveted the attention; it was fascinating.

Soccer was his passion. He loved to watch it and played it himself. Often, between meetings, he would drive to a soccer pitch and kick a ball around. In these impromptu matches, Ben Bella's closest companion was another enthusiastic soccer player, the foreign minister and one of the leading organizers of the plot against Ben Bella: Abdel Azis Buteflika.

Technically, the *coup* against Ben Bella was carried out with an absolutely flawless precision. The conditions were ideal: Villa Joly lay near Colonel Houari Boumedienne's house, and near the Villa Artur, where Buteflika lived, and above all near the *gendarmerie* barracks, the general staff head-quarters, where the plot was thrashed out. Ben Bella lived alone, surrounded by the houses of the very people who would later throw him into a dungeon. This was a drama that was literally played out in the backyard.

Ben Bella's house was watched by police and soldiers. At just after two in the morning, as the sentries went off-duty, they would have seen that the commander of the next shift was Tahar Zbiri, the chief of staff of the Algerian People's Army. Zbiri, the son of peasants, was a born military talent, a classic guerrilla type, who as a partisan commander in the liberation war distinguished himself by his unbelievable bravery and his splendid tactical thinking. After the liberation, Zbiri was marginalized by the élite of Boumedienne's army, and Ben Bella, guided by a foreboding—of which he may not even have been conscious—that Boumedienne might one day turn against him, raised Zbiri to chief of the general staff, believing apparently that in the event of a showdown with Boumedienne, Ben Bella could put Zbiri at the head of the army.

Yet it was Tahar Zbiri who, on the night of 19 June, led the operation. Several general staff officers took part, all wearing helmets and fatigues and carrying automatic rifles. They entered the Villa Joly. A pair of juggernauts, T-54 tanks, clanked along the Avenue Franklin Roosevelt.

The first thing Ben Bella must have seen when he woke was the rifle barrels pointed at him and then the massive but graceful silhouette of his friend, the hero of the liberation war—Zbiri, in whom the president had invested such great political hopes.

There are four different versions about what happened next; they are all journalistic invention. The only thing we can assume is that Ben Bella was led out of his bedroom. The rest is rumour.

Literally *nothing*, in fact, is known.

Ben Bella is said to have been killed. To have been wounded. To be alive. To have been not wounded, but ill.

Everything is reported, since nothing is known. One version has him on a ship anchored off Algiers. That version is confuted by a report that they are holding Ben Bella in the Sahara, at an army base. According to another view, he is still staying at the Villa Joly, which has a certain logic in that it would allow Boumedienne to keep Ben Bella under close observation. Boumedienne could be meeting with Ben Bella right now and negotiating.

Everything is possible, since nothing is known.

The most common version is the official one: that Ben Bella is in Algeria and being well treated. It might even be true.

Ben Bella was the leader of Algeria for three years.

Algeria is unique; at every moment it reveals its contrasts, its contradictions and its conflicts. Nothing is unambiguous and nothing fits into a formula.

Algeria is in that group of African countries where European colonialism lasted a long time. The French ruled Algeria for 132 years. Only the Portuguese in Angola and in Mozambique, and the Afrikaaners and English in South Africa, have had a longer colonial tenure. Algeria will bear the mark left by French colonial hegemony for decades. It has crippled and deformed Algeria—more so than in most of the other independent African countries—and in this deformation European settlers have played a major role. They always do. In assessing the devastation, what matters is not only the length of the colonial period, but, perhaps above all, the *number* of settlers: only South Africa has more. Around 1.2 million Europeans settled in Algeria, equal to the number of European settlers in all the twenty-six countries of tropical Africa combined. Settlers made up one tenth of the Algerian population.

There is another important factor: Algeria's geographical

position. Of all the African colonies, Algeria lay closest to its colonial metropolis. Today, it takes two hours to fly from Algiers to Paris, two hours that are not only a fact of communication but also a symbol of the bond between France and Algeria: one that the French developed over a period of 132 years and which neither the liberation war nor independence has severed. What's more, Algeria today is, as the statistics reveal, more closely bound (and not only economically) to its former colonial metropolis than any other independent country of Africa.

An image characteristic of a colonial country is the modern automated electronics factory, and beyond its walls are caverns inhabited by people who still use wooden hoes. 'Look what beautiful highways we've built for them,' say the colonialists. Indeed: but along those highways lie villages where people have yet to emerge from the palaeolithic age.

That is what you see in Algeria.

People who love France will rave about Algiers. It is a French city through and through, and even the Arab district of the Casbah has a French *esprit*. This is not Africa; it is Lyon, Marseille. International shop windows, sublime French cuisine, enchanting bistros. The contrivances of Parisian fashion reach here in a day, like the Parisian press and Parisian gossip.

But forty kilometres from Algiers, from this Paris of Africa, the stone age begins. After half an hour's drive I feel that I am back in Africa. Sixty kilometres from Algeria begin villages where to this day the people do not know the potter's wheel. The original Kabyle pots are formed by hand. And a new contrast: in this primitive Kabylia where they believe that washing children causes agonized death, I found a hospital where a Polish doctor who had just arrived from Kraków on a contract told me: 'They have an operating room here beyond my wildest dreams, with technical miracles I could never have imagined. I don't even know how to work these gadgets.'

A journey into the depths of Algeria is a journey in time, withdrawing into remote epochs that continue to exist here, still present, surrounded by the parched steppe or sands of the Sahara.

Nine tenths of Algeria is Sahara.

The Algerian Sahara is famous for the French atomic research centre at Reggane, for the first oil fields and for the stones of Tassilli where the oldest frescoes in the world have been preserved. At the town of Insalah in the Algerian Sahara the largest slave market in the world existed until recently: Ben Bella closed it, dividing the land and date palms of the slave traders among the slaves. Today Insalah is the only place in the world ruled by the slave class, known as the *haratin* (beasts of burden). Thus did Ben Bella make the dream of Spartacus come true.

Colonialism fosters social chasms, and the fissures still run through Algerian society. Colonial policy elevates a class of 'cultured' and 'reliable' natives while pushing the rest of society down on a stratum of poverty and ignorance. The bureaucrats, the bourgeois and the intelligentsia are cut off, all clearly and undemocratically raised above the rest of society. They have modelled themselves on the French, have adopted their way of living and, to a large degree, of thinking. Their habitat is the city, the desk vacated by the Frenchman, the café. Every Algerian politician is here from reactionaries to communists, united by their lifestyle, not their politics. The people who run Algeria's political and administrative machine have been recruited from these circles. A command of French is a condition for entry and these people are fluent in French. One more common characteristic: their isolation from the country. One thing these people are certainly not doing: they are not filling in the chasm between Algiers and Algeria. That is not their job; they do not think about it, mainly because they do not know the country: they live in Algiers, but they do not live in Algeria. 'It is striking,' someone told me in conversation, 'that these people are generally strangers to Algeria. Nobody here knows the countryside. Ben Bella took a slight interest in the villages, but nobody else.' And the villages are eighty per cent of Algeria.

The war in Algeria lasted seven and a half years and, with China's and Vietnam's, was one of the biggest wars of liberation of the last twenty years. The Algerian people showed the highest proof of their heroism, endurance and patriotism.

The war ended in defeat for France.

But Algeria paid a high price for their victory. It is still paying.

One tenth of the Algerian population—more than a million people—died in the war. The killed, the murdered, and the napalmed go by the name of *chuhada*—the martyred.

The French worked enormous destruction upon Algeria. Eight thousand villages were levelled, and millions were left without a roof over their head. Thousands of acres of forest, which shielded the soil from erosion, were burned. The cattle that provided half the peasantry with its livelihood were killed off (only three million head of cattle out of seven million survived). The *fellah* bore the brunt of the war.

The war caused huge migrations. Three million Algerians were driven from their villages and confined to reservations or resettled in the isolated regions. Four hundred thousand Algerians found themselves in prison or interned. Three hundred thousand fled to Tunisia and Morocco. At the same time, throughout the whole war, people from the villages—where repression hit hardest—fled to the cities, where, today, thirty per cent of the Algerian population now lives. Most of them have no jobs, but they do not want to go back to the villages, or they cannot return because the villages no longer exist.

Beyond the human and material losses, however, the traces of the war persist in the social consciousness. These are *living* traces, both positive and negative. Positive: because Algeria emerged from the war as a country of independent social and political ambitions, as an anti-imperialist and anti-colonial country. Negative: because divisions arose in Algerian society paralysing it.

This had never been a homogenous society. It consisted—and still consists—of a mix of ethnic groups, religious sects, social classes, tribes and clans: a rich and complex mosaic. The war introduced a certain order, drew the majority of Algerians into the struggle for a common goal; but as soon as the war ended, Algerian society began to disintegrate anew. But meanwhile, the war had added a new division: on one side, those who took part in the war: on the other side, those who served the French. And among those who took part were those who fought within the country and those who fought outside its borders.

Guerrillas fought inside the country. Three hundred thousand Algerians are estimated to have taken a direct part in the guerrilla war. They are the ones who shed the most blood. At the same time, the French were recruiting Algerians into its army and administration: their hands in the struggle against the rebels. The dividing line often ran through a single village, through a single family. ('Tujji does not contain one family,' writes Jules Roy about an

Algerian town in his book *The War in Algeria*, 'which would not have been split and which would not have had to come to terms with both the FLN [*Front de Libération National*] and the French army . . . In a certain family one man joined the rebels and another is in the French army . . . Why is he in the service of the French? Because there he receives a chunk of bread and a soldier's pay . . . Will these divisions vanish when peace comes? The army believes not, believes that on the contrary they will deepen . . . Is there any way not to share these fears? In Tujji, thirty men serve in the French army and every evening they lie in ambush for their guerrilla brothers.') The memory of who did what in the war remains alive in Algeria today. Today members of the Algerian professional class come from among the former collaborators, because only they had the opportunity to gain qualifications. Today they make up the administrative cadre: what's more, even though many of them are engaged in quiet but systematic sabotage, the government has also been forced to take them back into the army. During the conflict with Morocco, Algeria was losing because of the weakness of its support staff and finally concluded that it had to utilize the collaborators because they are the experts.

There is a third group: the emigrants—those who spent the war in French prisons (like Ben Bella) and those who served in the Algerian army that was formed in Morocco and Tunisia (like Boumedienne).

Algeria gained its independence during a profound crisis among members of the guerrilla movement: they had been bled dry, decimated, beaten back into the depths of the country, into the most desolate and inaccessible wasteland. They were being scattered. In the meantime, across the border in Tunisia and Morocco, a strong, expertly organized, excellently armed, well trained, solidly provisioned young Algerian army was forming. And as the guerrillas took a step towards seizing power, they found that the army had already rolled into Algeria with armoured columns and was enforcing a new order. From that moment in the summer of 1962 the border army has decided, still decides, and will continue to decide *everything* in Algeria.

From that moment too, the political activists, the whole élite that governs and the whole apparatus that administers will fall into three factions, three groups: emigrants, guerrilla veterans and collaborators.

This is the country that Ben Bella took over in 1962. He began under conditions that were not auspicious, the very same conditions that would determine his eventual defeat.

The country was weakened by the war, battered, particularly its villages, which were devastated. A million French colonists had fled in haste, and the country's own population was only starting to drift back from exile, from reservations, from the camps. The farms stood abandoned; the factories were idle. There was no organized administration, and members of a professional class were scarce, a technical cadre non-existent. Unemployment: universal. And, more than anything else, the society was exhausted, starved. It wanted peace; it wanted to eat. Even today, you can still feel clearly that this society is *tired*.

Ben Bella took power in a country that may be the most difficult land to govern in Africa. When he began, he was *alone*. A few months before, he had been in prison, having spent years in isolation. He arrived without a staff or troops. Most of the active politicians opposed him, blocked him; he was without a devoted and powerful party of his own. There was only one force from which Ben Bella could hope for backing in his struggle for power: the army, the masterful, confident border army of Boumedienne.

The essential feature of this army was that it was inactive. While the war was being fought inside Algeria, Boumedienne's army was unable to reach it because the army couldn't cross the network of impenetrable barriers along the border controlled by Tunisia and Algeria. Blocked in this way, Boumedienne's army became increasingly political, its political activity compensating for its inability to act militarily. In fact, all along, Boumedienne's soldiers trained on the revolutionary model, the soldier-political with a rifle in one hand and an agitprop manual in the other. The old guard of politicians gathered around the Algerian Provisional Government and FLN had seen the dangers for a long time: the old politicians, fearing the army, looked for ways to clip its wings, and on 2 July 1962, three days before Algerian independence, the Provisional Government decided to remove Boumedienne and the officers closest to him, who sit today on the Revolutionary Council. But Boumedienne was not about to be unseated. He came out openly against the old politicians. And Ben Bella too, whom the old politicians had refused to admit to power, stood against them. Logic led to Ben Bella allying with Boumedienne. Neither could do without the other. Ben Bella was a name, also at odds with the Provisional Government; he knew how to speak; he backed the idea of a politicized army. The politicized army, the only unified Algerian force at the end of the war, pushed Ben Bella into power. Only the army's candidate had a chance to take power. Only Ben Bella.

So it happened.

But at the same time, Ben Bella had from the beginning stepped into a snare: the army would be watching; the army knew that finally it could do whatever it wanted.

I want to defend Ben Bella just as I am going to defend Boumedienne. Ben Bella was not the 'demon' that the nervous, demagogic communiqué of 19 June accused him of being, no more than Boumedienne is the 'reactionary' that *L'Unita* wrote about. Both are victims of the same drama that every Third World politician lives through if he is honest, if he is a patriot. This was the drama of Lumumba and Nehru; it is the drama of Nyerere and Sekou Touré. The essence of the drama lies in the terrible *material resistance* that each one encounters on taking his first, second and third steps up the summit of power. Each one wants to do something good and begins to do it and then sees, after a month, after a year, after three years, that it just isn't happening, that it is slipping away, that it is bogged down in the sand. Everything is in the way: the centuries of backwardness, the primitive economy, the illiteracy, the religious fanaticism, the tribal blindness, the chronic hunger, the colonial past with its practice of debasing and dulling the conquered, the blackmail by the imperialists, the greed of the corrupt, the unemployment, the red ink. Progress comes with great difficulty along such a road. The politician begins to push too hard. He looks for a way out through dictatorship. The dictatorship then fathers an opposition. The opposition organizes a *coup*.

And the cycle begins anew.

Three years of Ben Bella's government.

The opposition accuses him of doing little.

Who says?

The balance sheet of his government has its indisputable credits: Ben Bella brought order to a country emerging from war; he got Algeria *moving*: the state apparatus, the economy, education, normal life. He turned over to the workers plantations and factories that the colonists had abandoned. Each time he nationalized an enterprise, it was an act of bravery. He prevented the civil war that was threatening the country and would have plunged it into a long decline. He prepared a programme of agricultural reform which changed the lives of several hundred thousand Algerian workers. He conferred on Algeria the prestige of becoming a leading country in the Third World, wanting Algeria to be the bridge between Europe and Africa. He opened Africa and the Arab world to the European left and to Communist parties. He was an active spokesman in the fight against colonialism.

Orthodoxy, fanaticism, did not burden Ben Bella's view of the world, which was open, receptive, tolerant, even if sometimes insufficiently discriminating. In his youth, Ben Bella had been a student of no ideological school and had joined the movement only because he wanted a free Algeria. He fought and was imprisoned. When he took power, his views seemed right wing, but then moved left, an unmistakable evolution, but an evolution that proceeded not from intellectual operations but rather somehow from his instincts, through practical politics. They say that Ben Bella's socialism was *sentimental*: they say that Ben Bella 'had his heart on the left,' that he simply *liked* socialism. Ben Bella tried to create the conditions in which youth could develop, to free the *fellah* from the tyranny of the magnates, to free slaves, to fight for the rights of women: Algerian women despaired when they heard that Ben Bella had been removed; they dressed in mourning. (One told me: 'He wanted to create a life for women. Now the men will lock us back up in the home.')

Ben Bella's socialism was brave and original. In simple terms, it was a socialist economy with the Islamic superstructure left undisturbed. The opposition accused him of talking too much and doing too little. They said that

Ben Bella's socialism was *verbal*.

How much time does the president of Algeria devote to fighting the opposition?

Ben Bella had a running battle with the opposition. Instead of developing his programme, he had to deal with his enemies. The situation is typically Algerian. Somebody is always plotting, and the constant threat of a *coup* paralyses the government. Take the year 1963. In April Ben Bella removes Khider, the general secretary of the FLN, because Khider has been organizing an opposition to him. In June he arrests Budiafy for conspiring against the government. In July the Kabyle leader Ait Ahmed announces that he has declared an open war against the government. In August Ben Bella removes Ferhat Abbas, the leader of the National Assembly, because Abbas opposes the party. In September he removes Rabeh Bitat for opposition activity; the same month he also removes Colonel el-Haji for organizing an uprising in Kabylia. In October and November there is a major rebellion among the Kabyle, who constitute nearly a fifth of the Algerian population. These are only the affairs that made headlines; how many conspiracies were nipped in the bud? How many small-time seditionists were there? In Algeria, nothing ever ends in a discussion. Political discipline is lacking, and the ability to think in terms of the good of the state is unknown. For that, you need years, whole generations.

Everything that occurs here is ideological, but the ideology is fluid, undefined, because this is not capitalism, which nobody espouses, and it is not socialism, which is known in only a cursory way, and it is not yet an Islamic orthodoxy. Some new quality is being born, and it is not yet expressed in any doctrine; everyone understands it in his own way. The Algerian mentality is full of clutter, contradictions and collages of the most fantastic incongruities. Political contentions are tortuous, as political opponents, operating without clear conceptions, can neither understand each other nor define their own positions. Their battles are fought on the ground of personal antagonism and old quarrels.

Nevertheless Ben Bella, with the members of the opposition gradually finding themselves behind bars or choosing to emigrate, seems to be picking his way skilfully through the labyrinth. Ben Bella thinks he is standing on solid ground.

Ben Bella is not standing on solid ground.

What was happening in Algeria just before the *coup*?

Things were not going well.

There were the problems that still needed to be solved: the millions of unemployed, the rural poverty, the confusion in the private sector, the lack of expertise, the gap between what the government said it would do for the country and its actual state, the deficit. Ben Bella could not solve these problems, and it was hard to see who would; it was hard to see when they could be solved.

Economic stagnation, internal disappointments, bureaucratic inertia, and the immobility of the masses always push Third World politicians in one of two directions: they become dictators or else they escalate their activities abroad, enlarge their foreign policy.

Ben Bella tried to make up for his domestic failures with a foreign policy that enhanced his prestige in the world. His policies attracted more and more of his time, more and more of his passion. He enjoyed visits and round table discussions. He could be captivating; people fell under the spell of his personal charm. His ambitions were great. He thought about supporting the rebels in Angola and

Mozambique; he trained South African guerrillas. He invited members of the World Youth Festival to Algiers. He made the capital the site for the second Afro-Asian conference. They say that he supervised the preparations personally, refusing to share them with *anyone*. Before the conference he was conducting wide-ranging correspondence with heads of state: he invited Chou En-Lai for a visit in June. He would set out on a visit to de Gaulle in July. Algeria became the pivotal Third World state, but the cost of its status—above all, the financial cost—was staggering. It ate up millions of dollars for which the country had a crying need.

Gradually, the gap between Ben Bella's domestic and foreign policies grew wider. The contrast deepened: Algeria had earned an international reputation as a revolutionary state; its policies were brave, decisive and dynamic; it had become a haven for the struggling and the oppressed of the world; it was an example for the non-European continents, a model, bright and entrancing: while at home, the country was stagnating; the unemployed filled the squares of every city; there was no investment; illiteracy ruled, bureaucracy, reaction, fanaticism ran riot; intrigues absorbed the attention of the government.

This gap between foreign and domestic politics, typical of many Third World countries, never lasts for long. The country, even if of the politician's making, always drags him back down to earth. The country cannot carry the burden of these policies. It cannot afford to; and it has no interest in them.

Two reasons confirmed the decision to go ahead with the coup: Ben Bella's style of governing and his preparations for a showdown with Boumedienne.

Like every autocrat, Ben Bella gradually dispensed with

people who thought independently and were prepared to defend their views, but, equally, could not respect and would not listen to those who remained. He dominated them; they were inferior. He paid less and less attention to those around him. He grew intolerant. He shouted at them. He no longer summoned them to help him make decisions. He summoned them to inform them of the decisions he had made. 'Today I've decided that so-and-so,' was how he would open politburo meetings. The principles of the court were at work, pushing the leader into a state of isolation. He held centre stage but held it alone. The Villa Joly gradually became empty. Ben Bella even lost touch with his old friends. He had no time for them, or they got on his nerves. If someone called on him to offer advice, Ben Bella would explode, ring for his bodyguards, and order them to arrest the caller. People began to stay out of his way, for fear of crossing him. He was a man of moods: he would easily fly into a rage and then he would sulk. He would get all wound up and stop thinking about what he was saying. Shortly before the *coup* he screamed at a cabinet meeting, 'I'm finished with all of you!'

He was indeed finished with them.

He no longer trusted anyone. People were either plotting or carrying out sabotage. One day he introduced Boumedienne to an Egyptian journalist with the words, 'This is the man who is preparing the conspiracy against me.' And he asked: 'How are the intrigues coming along?' 'Quite well, thank you,' Boumedienne replied.

He concentrated more and more power in his own hands. He was president of the republic and general secretary of the party. He also began taking over ministries. He decided who would be a member of the politburo, who would be a member of the central committee, who would join the government and sit in parliament. 'He decided everything,'

Buteflika later assured the journalists.

His was a complicated, many-layered personality, for, at the same time, he was trying to assure everyone that he liked them. He talked with each faction and made promises to each. In the morning he met with the leftists and made promises he could not keep; in the afternoon he met with the right wing and made more promises that he could not keep. People stopped believing him. The mutual suspicion grew, increasing the tension.

He played, he improvised. He was a great improviser, a tactician. But no clear strategic thinking guided his tactics. In these tactics there were no plans, there was only juggling.

Nobody could tell him anything. He was uncritical towards himself. He believed in his own strength, in his own star, in his own popularity. He had a good press—until the last minute he had a very good press. Writing anything bad about Ben Bella counted as a lapse of taste. Journalists liked him. He received them enthusiastically. He was so sure of himself that he felt the moment had come to deal with his main opponent, the very force that had carried him into power, that for three years had stood not so much behind him as beside him—the army. He did not know, he did not sense, the hopelessness of the struggle on which he was about to embark. The army was more than those in uniform: it was also those who had been in uniform, launching their careers. Half of the government, the central committee, the parliament, was army—present or past, *émigré* or guerrilla. The majority of Ben Bella's people belonged not to Ben Bella; they belonged to Boumedienne.

Ben Bella began by creating units of a people's militia, a counter-balance, he believed, to the influence of the army. It would not work. Next, while Boumedienne was in

Moscow, Ben Bella named Tahar Zbiri chief of the general staff, a move to which Boumedienne would never have agreed: Zbiri was not army; Zbiri had been a guerrilla.

They say that by the beginning of June the atmosphere had become unbearable, that Ben Bella was obviously preparing a purge. And then he himself declared his intentions.

A week before the *coup*, on Saturday 12 June, Ben Bella called for a politburo meeting the following Saturday, 19 June. Its agenda would be the following:

1. Changes in the cabinet.
2. Changes in the army command.
3. The liquidation of the military opposition.

Boumedienne was not present—he had already split irrevocably with Ben Bella—but half of the members of the politburo were Boumedienne's people anyway.

After this meeting, Ben Bella boarded an airplane and left for a week in Oran, leaving behind in Algiers everyone he had threatened.

Nobody knew who was to be dismissed. Everyone discreetly examined his conscience. Everyone felt uncertain, and the uncertainty united them. In Ben Bella's absence, discussions continued about whether to carry out the *coup*. Might it not be enough to just threaten a *coup*?

On Friday 18 June, a few hours before the *coup*, Ben Bella addressed a rally in Oran. He told the rally that 'Algeria is united as never before,' that all rumours of divisions in the government are nonsense, hostile propaganda. Afterwards he went to a soccer match—he never missed a match—and then he returned to Algeria in the late evening. Someone apparently telephoned him, requesting an emergency cabinet meeting. He answered that he was tired and was going to bed. At two in the morning he was awakened by his friend, Colonel Tahar Zbiri, who was wearing a helmet and holding an automatic.

Ben Bella disappeared without a trace.

The organizer of the *coup* was the first vice-premier, the minister of national defence, a member of the politburo of the FLN, a member of the Algerian National Assembly, the commander of the national people's army, and a former teacher of Arabic literature, Houari Boumedienne (born Bukharuba Mohammed). He was a colonel because the Algerian army, like all people's or revolutionary armies, has no rank of general or marshal. Officers' insignia are very modest, and the uniforms of privates and officers do not differ in the cut or the quality of the material.

Boumedienne is not photogenic (and, what's worse, the newspapers that dislike him retouch his face to give him a predatory cast), but in the flesh, he makes a likeable impression. He is of medium height, very slim, with a long, almost ascetic face, sunken cheeks and prominent jaws. His eyes, in deep sockets, are brown, mobile and uncommonly penetrating. Boumedienne does not look like an Arab. He has long, dark wavy hair and a close-cropped moustache rusty with the nicotine from his chain-smoking.

His manner astonished me. I met him a few days after the *coup* and was prepared for someone characterized by the mannerisms of a despot. In fact, Boumedienne was shy, embarrassed. I was attending a reception at the People's Palace. He bowed as low as a schoolboy to everyone. He did not know what to do with his hands, and his lack of social experience was obvious. After receiving the guests he sat in a chair against the wall and stared silently at an empty corner of the room. I do not know if he exchanged a single sentence with anyone in the course of the reception.

I asked one of the correspondents accredited in Algiers:

'Have any of you ever talked with Boumedienne?' Nobody had. 'He does not talk to anyone,' he said. 'He does not talk at all.' Indeed, Boumedienne is tightly sealed, a hermetic character: if Boumedienne has to say a word, he does so with great effort, as if he were laying bricks. He prefers to answer in monosyllables or with a nod of his head. He seldom delivers a speech. In the past year, he had given one speech. He reads his speeches from a text. They are always short, made up of dry theses. They say that Boumedienne treats civilians warily, that he cannot stand diplomatic chit-chat or round-table talks.

He comes across as a man who is always concentrating, absorbed by a particularly difficult and important idea. That is why he rarely smiles. He has none of a leader's stagecraft: he does not stroke children on the head or raise his hands in the air when he speaks or push himself forward in any way. He does not worry about his image or his status as a celebrity. This is not a pose, but the way he is. He dresses neglectfully; his long trouser cuffs wrinkle over his shoes; his jacket is buttoned the wrong way. He does not dress in a white shirt and tie; he always wears some sort of polo shirt, or fatigues.

He has one passion: the army; it is in his blood. He always howled when Ben Bella spent money on conferences and visits, because he wanted that money to go to the army. Boumedienne's world consists of barracks, staff and a firing range. Boumedienne's ambition is a political army, in the sense of the army-state. Saving the homeland: by means of the army. Development: by means of the army. Civilians never accomplish anything worthwhile; they mean demagogy and corruption; civilians always drag the country into a crisis. You need to have a few civilians in the government because the world does things that way, but only the army can keep the country on its feet, especially when the country is in a mess with factions eating at each other instead of thinking about the general good.

Boumedienne first met Ben Bella in Cairo, in 1954. Boumedienne was nothing at the time; he was twenty-eight years old and teaching in an Arabic school. Ben Bella pulled Boumedienne into the liberation struggle. Later Boumedienne carried Ben Bella into power, and in exchange Ben Bella defended Boumedienne against a party leadership that wanted the army to be only an army, to keep its nose out of politics. For years they did each other favours. They appeared everywhere together: Ben Bella, the born leader, the man of the world, in front; and behind him, like a shadow, silent, unmoving: Boumedienne.

Ben Bella and Boumedienne were two radically different characters, two entirely dissimilar mentalities. But each was indubitably an individual. Ben Bella had to get on Boumedienne's nerves, while Boumedienne had to strike fear into Ben Bella.

Boumedienne has a steely character. He is a man without hesitation, a revolutionary, an Arab nationalist, a spokesman for the Algerian *fellah* and the little man in the cities. Above all, Boumedienne will try to do something for these classes. They are the social elements to whose longings and ambitions the colonel is most sensitive and who make up ninety per cent of Algerian society.

The most common response to the *coup* in Algeria was distaste. Ambition was at work here. Algerians regard themselves as aristocrats among the Arabs, as cultured Arabs: there might be *coups* in places like Iraq or Libya, but not in Algeria. The *coup* compromised Algeria in the eyes of the world, especially as it fell in the week before the second Afro-Asian conference.

A *coup* here, with a couple of days to go before the

conference. Unbelievable confusion broke out. There was no reliable information. The Revolutionary Council was acting underground, like the Mafia. Nobody knew where the council was located or who was on the council. There was no official authority. Various figures would put themselves forward as spokesmen for the new order, but nobody knew them. Who could tell—he might be a spokesman or he might be some crackpot. Rumours circulated through the city. Ben Bella is alive. Ben Bella is dead. The conference will come off. There isn't going to be any conference. There's going to be a demonstration. There's going to be a revolt. Nasser is coming. Chou En-Lai is on his way. They're all coming. Nobody's coming. They're arresting the communists. They're arresting the Egyptians. They're arresting everybody. It has already started. It starts today. It starts tomorrow. It will start in a week.

A fearsome heatwave set in. People fainted in the streets. A rabid Ben Bella supporter told me: 'The people will not rise. It's too hot.' He was right: the days were quiet and the demonstrations began at night. They went on for five evenings. Young people, boys from the street came out, full of enthusiasm, caught up in it, but they were not organized. Two, perhaps three thousand people took part in the largest demonstrations in Algiers. The army was mustered against them. This army knows crowd control like the rosary. And it has the most modern equipment to enforce it. By the sixth day the demonstrations were over and the army returned to the barracks.

The young people apart, everything was quiet. The party was quiet; the labour unions were quiet; other organizations were quiet. People said that they were talking about what to do, that there was hesitation. The *coup* revealed the total fragmentation of society, the absence of cohesion, the

117

absence of bonds, the total absence of organized force.

Power lay on the side of the army. And the army was in control. The people of the left were pessimistic. They expected repression and slept, hidden in their homes. But the repression never came. Boumedienne did not lock up a single communist, a single leftist. The fear came from the fact that nobody in Algeria knows the army.

Boumedienne is not concerned with convincing people. Boumedienne acts. People in Africa like a leader who speaks, explains, confides. Nasser confided to the crowd at a rally that his daughter was not going to university because she failed her exams. He spoke about this sorrowfully, like the father of a child who had not succeeded; he spoke to thousands of fathers with similar problems.

The *coup* showed Algeria for what it is—a typical Third World country. On the bottom, there are the peasant masses on the eternal treadmill of poverty, in continual fear of a drought, praying constantly to Allah for the bowl of food that their barren land cannot supply them with. At the top, somewhere in the drawing rooms, someone is being locked up; someone has been overthrown. Two worlds—with no visible links between them.

After the *coup*, the Revolutionary Council took control in Algeria, the élite of the army making up the majority of the council.

There might have been a way to avoid the *coup*, which, as a tactical move, was extremely blunt. But it must be remembered that these were young people; by the standards of European politics, this is a youth organization. The average age of a Revolutionary Council member is somewhere between thirty-two and thirty-four. Boumedienne, at thirty-nine, is the senior member. Algerian politics is the domain of people in their twenties and

118

thirties. All of politics. What's more, these are Arabs, uncommonly proud people, sensitive on points of honour, hot-blooded, who will go after each other on the slightest pretext. 'Ben Bella offended us'—this is reason enough to lock Ben Bella up. Many of these flukes and freaks of African politics have this background: politics are practised by inexperienced people who have not yet learned to foresee the irrevocable consequences of their decisions, who have not yet absorbed the seriousness and prudence of older political war-horses.

On the African political stage, the army remains. Few in Algeria know what attitudes prevail in the army. There is something of the mafia about the army, and something of a religious sect. The officers do not greet each other with salutes; they shake hands and kiss each other on both cheeks.

People of various political orientations sit on the Revolutionary Council. Reactionaries and progressives, brought temporarily together by the fear of Ben Bella. There will be contention in this group, divisions and reclassifications will occur.

Anything can still happen: a new conspiracy, a new *coup*, revolt within the army, an uprising in Kabylia. Boumedienne told Heikal: 'The Algerian revolution is a revolution of surprises.'

A DISPUTE OVER A JUDGE ENDS IN THE FALL OF A GOVERNMENT

In November 1965 I was flying from Algiers to Accra. Along the way, the airplane landed in Conakry. The airport was filled with soldiers and police. I asked a man from Guinea what was going on. 'They've uncovered a conspiracy against the republic,' he said. 'There was an attempt on Sekou Touré's life. There have been arrests and resignations.'

In Accra, three days later, President Nkrumah called a press conference about Rhodesia. To reach his office, you had to pass through three gates and three courtyards. Each courtyard was filled with soldiers and police. We were told to arrive an hour before the press conference began and were then left standing in a line. One by one, we were admitted to a room where there were two policemen who carried out body searches. During the search, a policeman found a mechanical pencil in the pocket of my jacket. I was ordered to take it apart. I did so. I was ordered to put it together. I put it together. Take it apart again. The policemen conferred: there was something funny about that pencil. I had taken on a new role, the role of suspect, not knowing what the verdict would be. Finally, one of the policemen asked: 'Will you swear that this pencil cannot fire?' I answered yes, I would swear. They allowed me to take it.

Nkrumah looked tired. They say he is worn out and does not sleep well. In September, there were rumours in Accra that the army staff was forming a conspiracy, that the military might make a bid for power. At the end of September, Nkrumah removed the chief and assistant chief of the general staff, reorganized the ministry of defence and named himself commander-in-chief of the army. He received his marshal's baton at a special ceremony.

From Accra, I drove to Lagos in Nigeria. To get there, you cross through two small countries, Togo and Dahomey. Between Accra and the Ghanaian border, the road was closed six times and at each place there were army and police sentries standing in front of barriers, searching vehicles and inspecting documents.

At the border between Ghana and Togo there was a large padlocked gate, and when I drove up, a policeman wandered around it for a considerable time, looking for the key. Against this fence two years ago, Silvanus Olympio, the president of Togo, was executed by a firing squad of several officers. The capital of Togo, Lomé, begins just beyond the gate. It is small, sandy, hot and beautiful, a beach city and the sea can be felt everywhere. I listened to the radio news in the Hotel du Golf. The announcer read the first reports from Leopoldville about General Mobutu's *coup* in the Congo. Mobutu had arrested President Kasavubu and named himself president for five years. The most characteristic thing about Mobutu's speech was the precision of the decree that he would be president 'for five years'.

Nobody else would have anything to say about it.

But Mobutu was right: here it takes one officer and a thousand soldiers to establish a force that has no competition. Who can oppose them? How many governing parties are there here that in the moment of truth can field a thousand people who are dedicated, idealistic and, most important, not quarrelling with each other?

From Lomé to the border of Dahomey is fifty kilometres, a road runs beside the sea the whole way. Along the shore there is a fishing village, the longest village in the world, measuring more than a hundred kilometres in length, that begins in Ghana and ends in Dahomey. It was in Dahomey that I came across a *coup* by sheer accident.

As I was driving into Cotonou, which constitutes half the capital of Dahomey (the other half, called Port Novo, is thirty kilometres down the road), I passed a car being driven by the AFP correspondent, Jacques Lamoureux, who started shouting at me: 'Stop! Pull over! There's a revolution here!' Lamoureux was visibly elated, because Cotonou is a pretty little town but a boring one and its sole real attraction is the revolution, which occurs only once every few months.

This time the president of the republic, Sourou Migan Apithy, was locked in a struggle with Justin Ahomadegbe, the vice-president and head of the government. Their dispute had started with an argument over which one of them had the right to appoint a judge to the Supreme Court. Each wanted to fill the position, as each had a large family among whom various positions continually had to be distributed.

Little by little the argument between the president and the vice-president grew so heated that they had stopped talking to each other. They were in touch now only by correspondence, but even that was soon abandoned as well, since they returned again in the letters to the subject of the judge, and the name calling started all over. (Apithy showed me the letters later.)

For several months the state had ceased to function; the cabinet had not met; the country was paralysed.

Here we can see the mechanisms of African politics perfectly: Dahomey is a poor, underdeveloped country. To lift Dahomey out of poverty will require enormous effort, concentrated energy and education. But nobody is even working.

For months the government and the party, the parliament, the army, everything has been engaged in this dispute over a judge. There is relentless debate over the judge; resolutions are passed, various compromises are discussed.

I arrived in Cotonou on the day when both sides concluded that every legal argument had been exhausted and it was time to take concrete measures. Ahomadegbe struck first. He called a meeting of the politburo of the governing party, the PDD (*Parti Démocratique Dahoméen*), and the politburo voted to expel Apithy from the party and remove him from the presidency as 'the only means of saving the unity of the Dahomeyan nation.' That evening, Ahomadegbe went on the radio to say that history had given him responsibility for the fate of the Dahomeyan nation and, thus, he would take upon himself the duties of president. It looked therefore as if Ahomadegbe had won. But when we drove to Apithy's headquarters in Porto Novo the next day, we found him wholly unconcerned. Apithy ate dinner, had a nap and then received us and stated that he had been elected president by the people and only the people could deprive him of that office.

So Dahomey had two presidents, two heads of state.

Such a situation cannot go on for long. Fortunately, someone had the sense to call a meeting of political activists—something like a party convention—who were summoned to Cotonou on Sunday. This was the national leadership: party bosses, members of parliament, labour and youth movement officials, wholesalers from the bazaar (an important political force), priests, witch-doctors and army officers. The meeting took place in the palace of the former president of Dahomey, Hubert Maga, who was overthrown by the army in 1963.

The palace is famous.

The building of it used up all of the funds that had been set aside for the three-year national development plan. Its huge gates are carved of pure gold. Snakes, also gold, twine

124

around the marble columns in the main hall. The whole palace drips gold. Niches in the walls are inlaid with precious stones, and authentic Persian carpets cover the floors. During the confusion of 1963, when Colonel Christopher Soglo overthrew President Hubert Maga, the precious silver dishes that Maga had imported from Paris antique shops disappeared. Vice-President Ahomadegbe took it upon himself to investigate, and concluded publicly that Colonel Soglo's wife had taken the silver. The government crisis that subsequently erupted was smoothed over somehow, but it was clear that if Soglo got involved now—decided to act—Ahomadegbe would have to lose.

In any case, we went to the meeting.

On the steps of the palace we met Soglo, now a general, who greeted us and stopped to talk. Soglo is a stocky, jovial, energetic man. He is fifty-six. He served in the French army from 1931 as a career NCO. He was dressed simply, in an army shirt without insignia. He wore a green beret. Soglo did not carry a weapon, and neither did other officers, nor the paratroopers surrounding the palace. During the course of the military takeover that I was about to witness, I did not see a single armed soldier. This distinguished the present *coup* from that of October 1963, when the army used weapons: namely, the one mortar in the possession of the Dahomeyan army. When Soglo arrested Hubert Maga, the members of the cabinet, unsure about what was happening, barricaded themselves in a small building near the main square. Soglo himself then set up the mortar in front of the building (he was the only one in the army who knew how to operate it) and announced through a megaphone that if the cabinet did not resign by four in the afternoon, he would begin firing on the building. The cabinet decided unanimously to resign, which it communicated to Soglo through the window, and thus ended the political crisis of October 1963.

Now Soglo stood with us on the stairs of the palace, in a good humour, conversing. He told us that he was completely unable to reconcile them—'them' meaning the self-proclaimed president and the one elected by the people. Later he added that he would 'have to do something.'

Just before the party convention opened, word went around that the witch-doctors had come out in support of Ahomadegbe. 'Well, Apithy's finished,' opined the AFP correspondent, Jacques Lamoureux, who then sent a dispatch to Paris saying so. But we waited. The convention ended without an agreement later that afternoon, with the activists splitting into two camps, supporting different presidents. In the evening flyers were handed out, consisting of three sentences: 'Down with Fascism! Down with Ahomadegbe! Long live the Army!' That same evening, Ahomadegbe made a dramatic, single-handed attempt to arrest Apithy. He drove to Porto Novo, where Apithy resided. He then went to the *gendarmerie* barracks and demanded that the commander of the *gendarmes*, Major Jackson, arrest Apithy. But the major told Ahomadegbe that he took orders from General Soglo; the two argued, then Ahomadegbe went back to Cotonou. The major must then have reported everything to General Soglo, because, by the time Ahomadegbe had returned, Soglo had decided to act at once.

That same night, at four in the morning, Soglo woke Apithy and ordered him to sign his letter of resignation. Apithy said that he would sign only if he saw with his own eyes that Ahomadegbe had also signed a letter of resignation. Soglo agreed, got into his car and drove to Cotonou. He woke Ahomadegbe and ordered him to sign his resignation. Ahomadegbe signed. Soglo took the paper and drove back to Porto Novo, to Apithy. The whole time,

Soglo was alone. He showed Ahomadegbe's resignation to Apithy. Then Apithy signed his own resignation. By six in the morning, the crisis was over. Soglo named a new premier: Tairu Congacu, a colourless, second-rank figure. Soglo obviously kept the real power in his own hands.

From this revolt in Dahomey I drove straight into the fires of the civil war that had been going on in western Nigeria since October. On the road from the Dahomey–Nigeria border to Lagos: barriers, police, troops, searches, checkpoints. Burned cars in the ditches. Burned huts in the villages. Army patrols in trucks. This war was hopeless and absurd, with no end in sight. Hundreds of people had already died, hundreds of houses had been burned and great sums of money wasted.

In the course of one month I had driven through five countries. In four of them, there were states of emergency. In one, the president had just been overthrown; in a second, the president had saved himself only by chance; in a third, the head of government was afraid to leave his house, which was surrounded by troops. Two parliaments had been dissolved. Two governments had fallen. Scores of political activists had been arrested. Scores of people had been killed in political conflicts.

Over a distance of 520 kilometres, I had been checked twenty-one times and subjected to four body searches. Everywhere there was an atmosphere of tension, everywhere the smell of gunpowder.

THE BURNING ROADBLOCKS

January 1966. In Nigeria a civil war was going on. I was a correspondent covering the war. On a cloudy day I left Lagos. On the outskirts police were stopping all cars. They were searching the trunks, looking for weapons. They ripped open sacks of corn: could there be ammunition in that corn?

Authority ended at the city line.

The road leads through a green countryside of low hills covered with a close, thick bush. This is a laterite road, rust-coloured, with a treacherous uneven surface.

These hills, this road and the villages along it are the country of the Yorubas, who inhabit south-western Nigeria. They constitute a quarter of Nigeria's population. The heaven of the Yorubas is full of gods and their earth full of kings. The greatest god is called Oduduwa and he lives at a height higher than the stars, higher even than the sun. The kings, on the other hand, live close to the people. In every city and every village there is a king.

In 1962 the Yorubas split into two camps. The overwhelming majority belongs to the UPGA (United Progressive Grand Alliance); an insignificant minority belongs to the NNDP (Nigerian National Democratic Party). Owing to the trickery of the Nigerian central government, the minority party rules the Yorubas' province. The central government prefers a minority government in the province as a way of controlling the Yorubas and curbing their separatist ambitions: thus has the party of the overwhelming majority, the UPGA, found itself in opposition. In the autumn of 1965 there were elections in the Yorubas' province. It was obvious that the majority party, UPGA, had won. Nevertheless, the central government, ignoring the results and the sentiments of the Yorubas, declared the victory of the puppet NNDP, which went on to form a government. In protest, the majority party created its own government. For a time there were two governments. In the end, the members of the majority government were imprisoned, and the UPGA declared open war against the minority government.

And so we have misfortune, we have a war. It is an unjust, dirty, hooliganish war in which all methods are allowed—whatever it takes to knock out the opponent and gain control. This war uses a lot of fire: houses are burning, plantations are burning, and charred bodies lie in the streets.

The whole land of the Yorubas is in flames.

I was driving along a road where they say no white man can come back alive. I was driving to see if a white man could, because I had to experience everything for myself. I know that a man shudders in the forest when he passes close to a lion. I got close to a lion so that I would know how it feels. I had to do it myself because I knew no one could describe it to me. And I cannot describe it myself. Nor can I describe a night in the Sahara. The stars over the Sahara are enormous. They sway above the sand like great chandeliers. The light of those stars is green. Night in the Sahara is as green as a Mazowsze meadow.

I might see the Sahara again and I might see the road that carried me through Yoruba country again. I drove up a hill and when I got to the crest I could see the first flaming roadblock down below.

It was too late to turn back.

Burning logs blocked the road. There was a big bonfire in the middle. I slowed down and then stopped; it would have been impossible to have carried on. I could see a dozen or so young people. Some had shotguns, some were holding knives and the rest were armed with machetes.

They were dressed alike in blue shirts with white sleeves, the colours of the opposition, of the UPGA. They wore black and white caps with the letters UPGA. They had pictures of Chief Awolowo pinned to their shirts. Chief Awolowo was the leader of the opposition, the idol of the party.

I was in the hands of UPGA activists. They must have been smoking hashish because their eyes were mad and they did not look fully conscious. They were soaked in sweat, seemed possessed, frenzied.

They descended on me and pulled me out of the car. I could hear them shouting 'UPGA! UPGA!' On this road, UPGA ruled. UPGA held me in its sway. I could feel three knife-points against my back and I saw several machetes (these are the Africans' scythes) aimed at my head. Two activists stood a few steps away, pointing their guns at me in case I tried to get away. I was surrounded. Around me I could see sweaty faces with jumpy glances; I could see knives and gun barrels.

My African experience had taught me that the worst thing to do in such situations is to betray your despair; the worst thing is to make a gesture of self-defence, because that emboldens them, because that unleashes a new wave of aggression in them.

In the Congo when they poked machine-guns in our bellies, we could not flinch. The most important thing was keeping still. Keeping still takes practice and willpower, because everything inside screams that you should run for it or jump the other guy. But they are always in groups and that means certain death. This was a moment when he, the black, was testing me, looking for a weak spot. He would have been afraid of attacking my strong point—he had too much fear of the white in him—so he looked for my weakness. I had to cover all my weaknesses, hide them somewhere very deep within myself. This was Africa, I was in Africa. They did not know that I was not their enemy. They knew that I was white, and the only white they had known was the colonizer, who abased them, and now they wanted to make him pay for it.

The irony of the situation was that I would die out of responsibility for colonialism; I would die in expiation of the slave merchants; I would die to atone for the white planter's whip; I would die because Lady Lugard had ordered them to carry her in a litter.

The ones standing in the road wanted cash. They wanted me to join the party, to become a member of UPGA and to pay for it. I gave them five shillings. That was too little, because somebody hit me on the back of the head. I felt pain in my skull. In a moment there was another blow. After the third blow I felt an enormous tiredness. I was fatigued and sleepy; I asked how much they wanted.

They wanted five pounds.

Everything in Africa was getting more expensive. In the Congo soldiers were accepting people into the party for one pack of cigarettes and one blow with a rifle butt. But here I had already got it a couple of times and I was still supposed to pay five pounds. I must have hesitated because the boss shouted to the activists, 'Burn the car!' and that car, the Peugeot that had been carrying me around Africa, was not mine. It belonged to the Polish state. One of them splashed gasoline on to the Peugeot.

I understood that the discussion had ended and I had no way out. I gave them the five pounds. They started fighting over it.

But they allowed me to drive on. Two boys moved the burning logs aside. I looked around. On both sides of the road there was a village and the village crowd had been watching the action. The people were silent; somebody in the crowd was holding up a UPGA banner. They all had photographs of Chief Awolowo pinned on their shirts. I liked the girls best. They were naked to the waist and had the name of the party written across their breasts: UP on the right breast, and GA on the left one.

I started off.

I could not turn back; they allowed me only to go forward. So I kept driving through a country at war, a cloud of dust behind me. The landscape was beautiful here, all vivid colours, Africa the way I like it. Quiet, empty—every now and then a bird taking flight in the path of the car. The roaring of a factory was only in my head. But an empty road and a car gradually restore calm.

Now I knew the price: UPGA had demanded five pounds of me. I had less than five pounds left, and fifty kilometres to go. I passed a burning village and then an emptying village, people fleeing into the bush. Two goats grazed by the roadside and smoke hung above the road.

Beyond the village there was another burning roadblock.

Activists in UPGA uniforms, knives in their hands, were kicking a driver who did not want to pay his membership fee. Nearby stood a bloody, beaten man—he hadn't been able to come up with the dues, either. Everything looked like the first roadblock. At this one, though, I hadn't even managed to announce my desire to join UPGA before I received a pair of hooks to the midsection and had my shirt torn. They turned my pockets inside out and took all my money.

I was waiting for them to set me on fire, because UPGA was burning many people alive. I had seen the burnt corpses. The boss at this roadblock popped me one in the face and I felt a warm sweetness in my mouth. Then he poured benzene on me, because here they burn people in benzene: it guarantees complete incineration.

I felt an animal fear, a fear that struck me with paralysis; I stood rooted to the ground, as if I was buried up to the neck. I could feel the sweat flowing over me, but under my skin I was as cold as if standing naked in sub-zero frost.

I wanted to live, but life was abandoning me. I wanted to live, but I did not know how to defend my life. My life was going to end in inhuman torment. My life was going to go out in flames.

What did they want from me? They waved a knife before my eyes. They pointed it at my heart. The boss of the operation stuffed my money into his pocket and shouted at me, blasting me with his beery breath: 'Power! UPGA must get power! We want power! UPGA is power!' He was shaking, swept up in the passion of power; he was mad on power; the very word 'power' sent him into ecstasy, into the highest rapture. His face was flooding sweat, the veins on his forehead were bulging and his eyes were shot with blood and madness. He was happy and he began to laugh in joy. They all started laughing. That laughter saved me.

They ordered me to drive on.

The little crowd around the roadblock shouted 'UPGA!' and held up their hands with two fingers stretched out in the 'V' sign: Victory for UPGA on all fronts.

About four kilometres down the road the third roadblock was burning. The road was straight and I could see the smoke a long way off, and then I saw the fire and the activists. I could not turn back. There were two barriers behind me. I could only go forward. I was trapped, falling out of one ambush and into another. But now I was out of money for ransom, and I knew that if I didn't pay up they would burn the car. Above all, I didn't want another beating. I had been whipped, my shirt was in tatters and I reeked of benzene.

There was only one way out: to run the roadblock. It was

risky, because I might wreck the car or it might catch fire. But I had no choice.

I floored it. The roadblock was a kilometre ahead. The speedometer needle jumped: 110, 120, 140. The car shimmied and I gripped the wheel more tightly. I leaned on the horn. When I was right on top of it I could see that the bonfire stretched all the way across the road. The activists were waving their knives for me to stop. I saw that two of them were winding up to throw bottles of gasoline at the car and for a second I thought, so, this is the end, this is the end, but there was no turning back. There was no turning . . .

I smashed into the fire, the car jumped, there was a hammering against the belly pan, sparks showered over the windshield. And suddenly—the roadblock, the fire and the shouting were behind me. The bottles had missed. Hounded by terror, I drove another kilometre and then I stopped to make sure the car wasn't on fire. It wasn't on fire. I was all wet. All my strength had left me; I was incapable of fighting; I was wide open, defenceless. I sat down on the sand and felt sick to my stomach. Everything around me was alien. An alien sky and alien trees. Alien hills and manioc fields. I couldn't stay there, so I got back in and drove until I came to a town called Idiroko. On the way I passed a police station and I stopped there. The policemen were sitting on a bench. They let me wash and straighten myself out.

I wanted to return to Lagos, but I couldn't go back alone. The commandant started to organize an escort. But the policemen were afraid to travel alone. They needed to borrow a car, so the commandant went into town. I sat on a bench reading the *Nigerian Tribune*, the UPGA paper. The paper was dedicated to party activities and the party's fight for power. 'Our furious battle,' I read, 'is continuing.

For instance, our activists burned the eight-year-old pupil Janet Bosede Ojo of Ikerre alive. The girl's father had voted for the NNDP.' I read on: 'In Ilesha the farmer Alek Aleke was burned alive. A group of activists used the "Spray-and-Lite" method [also known as 'UPGA candles'] on him. The farmer was returning to his fields when the activists grabbed him and commanded him to strip naked. The farmer undressed, fell to his knees and begged for mercy. In this position he was sprayed with benzene and set afire.' The paper was full of similar reports. UPGA was fighting for power, and the flames of that struggle were devouring people.

The commandant returned, but without a car. He designated three policemen to ride in mine. They were afraid to go. In the end they got in, pointed their rifles out the windows, and we drove off that way, as if in an armoured vehicle. At the first roadblock the fire was still burning but there was nobody in sight. The next two roadblocks were in full swing, but when they saw the police they let us through. The policemen weren't going to allow the car to be stopped; they didn't want to get into a fight with the activists. I understood—they lived here and they wanted to survive. Today they had rifles, but usually they went unarmed. Many policemen had been killed in the region.

At dusk we were in Lagos.

The Plan of the Never-Written Book that Could Be, Etc.

31

God's victim, I have been lying in Lagos for two months now like Lazarus, struggling against illness. It is some sort of tropical infection, blood poisoning or a reaction to an unknown venom, and it is bad enough to make me swell up and leave my body covered with sores, suppurations and carbuncles. I have no strength left to fight the pain, so I ask Warsaw for permission to return. I have often been sick in Africa, since the tropics beget everything in excess, in exaggeration, and the law of intensified propagation and variety applies to bacteria and infections. There is no way out: if you want to enter the most sombre, treacherous and untrodden recesses of this land, you have to be prepared to pay the reckoning with your health, if not your life. Yet every hazardous passion is like this: a Moloch that wants to devour you. In this situation, some opt for a paradoxical state of existence—so that, on arriving in Africa, they disappear into luxurious hotels, never venture outside the pampered neighbourhoods of the whites, and, in short, despite finding themselves geographically in Africa, they continue to live in Europe—except that it's a substitute Europe, reduced and second-rate. Indeed, such a lifestyle does not agree with the authentic traveller and lies beyond the means of the reporter, who must experience everything at his own cost.

32

More devastating than malaria or amoebas, fevers or

contagion is the disease of loneliness, the disease of the tropical depression. Defending yourself against it takes iron resistance and a strong will. Yet even then it is not easy. (Here begin a description of the depression.) Describe the extremities of fatigue after empty days that pass purposelessly. Afterwards the sleepless nights, the morning listlessness, the slow immersion in sticky, clotting mucus, in an unpleasant and repulsive fluid. Now you look at yourself with loathing. Now you are repulsively white. The flavourless, unappetizing whiteness. Chalky, waxy, freckled, mottled, blood-blistered white skin—in this climate, in this sun! Horrible! In addition, everything is sweaty: head, back, belly, buttocks, all as if it had been left under a tap that had been carelessly turned-off so that there is a continuous—emphasize that, *continuous*—dripping of a warm, colourless, insistently sharp-smelling fluid. Sweat.

'Oh, I see that you perspire a great deal.'

'Yes, ma'am, and yet it's healthy. Perspiration in the tropics is, if you will, health. Whoever perspires can bear the climate. It won't wear him out.'

'And you know, I simply can't perspire. A little bit, of course, but it's really nothing. I can't imagine why.'

'To perspire you need to drink a lot. Drink and drink, whatever is available. Juices, soft drinks and a little alcohol do you some good, too. It's better to perspire than to urinate. The kidneys work less.' Oh, God, those endless conversations about sweat, until the ears burn.

'But it's a natural thing. Perspiring isn't shameful.'

'And you know, there's something psychological to it, too. If you point out to someone that he is perspiring, he immediately begins perspiring even more.'

'You're right, ma'am. At this moment, I've just started dripping with perspiration.'

Thank you, sir and madam, for the conversation—

and you think: poor white people overwhelmed by the tropics, thrashing about in the tropics like fish on the beach, packed together, flaccid, crumpled, wrung out and, precisely, sweaty (she less, he more). Describe the characteristic sweat complex, which is in fact a weakness complex.

In the tropics the white feels weakened, or downright weak, whence comes the heightened tendency to outbursts of aggression. People who are polite, modest or even humble in Europe fall easily into rage here, get into fights, destroy other people, start feuds, fall prey to megalomania, grow touchy about their prestige and significance and go around completely devoid of self-criticism, bragging about the position and the influence they have at home. From the summits of fancied authority they swear vengeance upon their enemies (and the enemy is no imperialist politician, but the ordinary co-worker at the next desk) and if someone told them that they ought to have their head examined (which I often felt like doing) they would be mortally offended. People make spectacles of themselves without even thinking about it. But then again, if it were otherwise there would be no literature. Writers would have nothing to observe. All of it—the weakness and the aggression, the loathing and the mania—is a product of the tropical depression that is also symptomized by wild swings of emotion. Here are two friends sitting at the bar for several hours, drinking beer. Through the windows they can see the waves of the Atlantic, palms, girls on the beach. None of it means anything to them. They are sunk in depression; they have wall eyes, pained spirits, atrophied bodies. They are silent and will remain completely listless all evening. Suddenly one of them picks up his mug and slams the other one across the head. Screams, blood and the thump of a body hitting the floor. What was it? Exactly nothing. Or rather, the following occurred: the depression torments you and you try to free yourself of it. But the requisite strength is not born in a moment. It takes time to accumulate it in sufficient quantity to overcome the depression. You drink beer and wait for that blessed moment. And there is a further pathological deviation evoked by the action of the tropics. Namely, in the period leading up to the blessed moment in which you will be able to overcome the depression calmly and with dignity, a surplus of strength arises in you—no one knows from where—a surplus that blows up and assaults the brain in a wave of blood, and in order to vent that surplus you have to crack your innocent friend across the skull. This is the depressive explosion—a phenomenon known to all habitués of the tropics. If you are the witness of such a scene, you need not step in—there is no further reason to do so: that one blow frees a person of the surplus and he is now a normal, conscious individual, free of the depression. Describe other behaviour from periods of depression. Physiological changes in chronic states: the slumber of cortical cells, the numbness in the fingertips, the loss of sensitivity to colours and the general dulling of vision, the transient loss of hearing. There would be a lot to say.

33

At the beginning of the 1960s Africa was a fascinating world. I wrote volumes about it (I haven't mentioned that the press agencies insist on a correspondent's writing and writing, without pause, without stopping for breath—I don't want to say without thinking, even though such a prospect is also possible from time to time—that they demand constant telexes, dispatches, some by post or with returning travellers, an unending stream of information, commentary, reporting, opinions and evaluations, because only when the folios full of his collected correspondence are breaking at the seams and spilling out of the cabinets back at the home office can he count on their saying approvingly: That one's all right. He's really good). I too wrote volumes of information and commentary, of which not a trace remains. But our job is like a baker's work—his rolls are tasty as long as they're fresh; after two days they're stale; after a week they're covered with mould and fit only to be thrown out.

34

Some time after sending the 'Burning Roadblocks' piece to Warsaw, I received a telegram from my boss Michal Hofman, then the managing editor of the Polish Press Agency. 'I kindly request,' I read in the telegram, 'that once and for all you put an end to these exploits that could end in tragedy.' The once and for all referred to previous predicaments that I really might not have been able to get out of. My boss treated me with patience and understanding. He tolerated my adventures and my pathological lack of discipline. At my most irresponsible I would suddenly break contact with Warsaw without having told them my plans and would disappear without a trace: throw myself into the jungle, float down the Niger in a dugout, wander through the Sahara with nomads. The main office, not knowing what had happened or how to look for me, would, as a last resort, send telegrams to various embassies. Once, when I showed up in Bamako, our embassy there showed me a telegramme: 'Should Kapuściński happen to show up in your territory, please inform PAP through the Ministry of Foreign Affairs.'

35

In Lagos, when I was ill, I read through *Tristes Tropiques*. Claude Lévi-Strauss has been staying in the Brazilian jungles, carrying out ethnographic research among the Indian tribes. He is running into difficulties and resistance from the Indians; he is discouraged and exhausted.

Above all, he asks himself questions: Why has he come here? With what hopes or what objectives? Is this a normal occupation like any other profession, the only difference being that the office or laboratory is separated from the practitioner's home by a distance of several thousand kilometres? Or does it result from a more radical choice, which implies that the anthropologist is calling into question the system in which he was born and brought up? It was now nearly five years since I had left France and interrupted my university career. Meanwhile, the more prudent of my former colleagues were beginning to climb the academic ladder: those with political leanings, such as I had once had, were already members of parliament and would soon be ministers. And here was I, trekking across desert wastes in pursuit of a few pathetic human remnants. By whom or by what had I been impelled to disrupt the normal course of my existence? Was it a trick on my part, a clever diversion, which would allow me to resume my career with additional advantages for which I would be given credit? Or did my decision express a deep-seated incompatibility with my social setting so that, whatever happened, I would inevitably live in a state of ever greater estrangement from it? Through a remarkable paradox, my life of adventure, instead of opening up a new world to me, had the effect rather of bringing me back to the old one, and the world I had been looking for disintegrated in my grasp. Just as, once they were in my power, the men and the landscapes I had set out to conquer lost the significance I had hoped they would have for me, so for these disappointing yet present images, other images were substituted which had been held in reserve by my past and had seemed of no particular importance when they still belonged to the reality surrounding me. Travelling through regions upon which few eyes had gazed, sharing the existence of communities whose poverty was the price—paid in the first instance by them—for my being able to go back thousands of years in time, I was no longer fully aware of either world. What came to me were fleeting visions of the French countryside I had cut myself off from, or snatches of music and poetry which were the most conventional expressions of a culture which I must convince myself I had renounced, if I were not to belie the direction I had given to my life. On the plateau of the western Mato Grosso, I had been haunted for weeks, not by the things that lay all around me and that I would never see again, but by a hackneyed melody, weakened still further by the deficiencies of my memory—the melody of Chopin's Etude no. 3, opus 10, which, by a bitterly ironical twist of which I was well aware, now seemed to epitomize all I had left behind.

36

Consent for my return home arrived and I went from Lagos straight to a hospital bed on Plocka Street. In the small, suffocatingly, overcrowded ward lay perhaps fifteen people, two of whom died before my eyes. The rest snored, moaned, argued or went on and on about the war. The window looked out on a lifeless courtyard bordered by the wall of the morgue, a grey muslin sky in which the sun never appeared and a bare tree that looked like a broom handle that a janitor had stuck in snow before wandering off for a vodka. Even so, I liked it there.

37

I returned to the editorial offices (it was the beginning of 1967) but had no idea of what to do. I felt smashed inside, shattered; I wasn't suited for anything; I wasn't in touch; I wasn't there. I did not regard my stay in Africa as merely a job. I had gone there after years of having to function as a cog in a complex mechanism of instructions and commands, theses and guidelines, and Africa had been, for me, liberation, where—between 37°21' and 34°52' latitude and 17°32' and 51°23' longitude, between Rass Ben Sekka in the north and Needle Point in the south, between Capo Almadi in the west and Raas Xaafun in the east—I had left part of myself behind. Africa was a film that kept playing, an unbroken loop, non-stop, in show after show, but nobody around me cared about what was happening in my cinema. People were talking about who had taken whose place in Koszalin, or arguing about some television programme in which Cwiklińska had been first-rate, although others said she hadn't been, or giving each other merry advice about how you can travel to Bulgaria for a holiday inexpensively and actually make money as well. I didn't know the man who had gone to Koszalin, I hadn't seen that programme on television and I had never been in Bulgaria. The worst thing was the acquaintances I would run into on the street who would begin by saying, 'What are you doing here?' Or,

'Haven't you left yet?' I understood: they did not regard me as one of their own. Life was going on and they were swimming in its current. Talking about something, arranging something, cooking something up, but I didn't know what, they weren't telling me, they weren't expecting me to go along with them; they weren't trying to win me over. I was an outsider.

38

At the editorial offices they could tell that I was hanging around the corridors without purpose or goal. In principle it is accepted that when a correspondent returns from a bureau in the field he has no assignment or work for a certain time and becomes a fifth wheel to our long-suffering, dedicated team. But my alienated behaviour and prolonged idleness had exceeded all the limits of tolerance, and Hofman decided to do something with me. Thus there was an attempt—one of a series in my life—to establish me behind a desk. My boss led me to a room containing a desk and a typist and said, 'You're going to work here.' I looked it over: the typist—yes, she was nice; the desk—abominable. It was one of those small desks, a mousetrap, which sit by the thousands in our cluttered and overcrowded offices. Behind such a desk, a man resembles an invalid in an orthopaedic brace. He cannot stand up normally to shake hands, but must first disengage himself delicately from his chair and cautiously rise, attending more to the desk than the visitor, as it takes only a nudge for this rickety, spindly-legged contraption to collapse with a roar on to the parquet. The seriousness of a whole office disintegrates into sniggering when instead of an official enthroned behind a monumental sculptured desk it sees a crouching, cramped wretch imprisoned in a miniature cut-rate snare. I cannot suffer a desk! I have never had a desk, and I have never joined in at meetings where people shout into each other's faces and jump down each other's throats with a desk between them. In general I am no enthusiast of furniture and regard as the ideal house the Japanese one in which there is nothing besides the walls, the ceiling, the floor and the ichiban. Furniture divides man from man; people cower behind furniture as though behind barricades; they disappear into furniture like birds into holes. If someone shows me a time-honoured antique and announces ceremoniously that it comes from this or that century and epitomizes such and such a style, I am unmoved. Nevertheless, I understand the utilitarian value of furniture, the need for it, its awkward if practical vocation in the interest of human comfort. This tolerance of mine extends to all furniture except the desk. Upon the desk, I have declared a silent war. It is, after all, a specific piece of furniture with particular properties. While many whole categories of furniture may be man's serviceable instruments, his slaves, in the case of the desk a contrary relationship obtains: man is its instrument, its slave. Many thinkers worry over the progressive bureaucratization of the world and the social threat of its terror. Yet they forget that these very bureaucrats are themselves terrorized, and that they are terrorized by their desks. Once plunked down behind one, a man will never learn to tear himself free. The loss of his desk will strike him as a natural disaster, a catastrophe, a fall into the abyss. Notice how many people commit suicide at their desks, how many are carried straight from their desks to psychiatric hospitals, how many suffer their heart attacks behind desks. Whoever sits down behind a desk begins to think differently; his vision of the world and his hierarchy of values change. From then on he will divide humanity into those who have desks and those who do not, and into significant owners of desks and insignificant ones. He will now see his life as a frenzied progress from a small desk to a larger one, from a low desk to a higher one, from a narrow desk to a wider desk. Once ensconced behind a desk he masters a distinct language and knows things—even if yesterday, deskless, he knew nothing. I have lost many friends for reasons of desks. Once they were truly close friends. I cannot say what demon it is that slumbers in a man and makes him talk differently once he's set behind a desk. Our symmetrical, brotherly relations fall apart; there arises a troublesome and asymmetrical division into higher and lower, a pecking order that makes us both feel uncomfortable, and there is no way to reverse the process. I can tell that the desk already has him in its clutches, in a full nelson. After a few experiments I give up and quit calling. Both of us, I think, accept the outcome with relief. From then on I have known that whenever one of my friends starts achieving ever more showy desks, he is lost to me. I avoid him to spare myself the lurch that marks every transition from symmetry to asymmetry in human relationships. Sometimes a man will get up from behind his desk to walk down and talk with you at the other end of his office, in a couple of armchairs or at a round table. Such a person knows what desks are and knows that a chat between people divided by one is like a discussion between a sergeant perched in the turret of a tank and a raw frightened recruit standing at attention and looking right into the barrel of the big gun.

39

So even if the desk my editor had placed me behind had an inlaid mother-of-pearl top, I had to get out. The desk after all, has one more dangerous property: it can serve as an instrument of self-justification. I sense this in moments of crisis, when I can't get anything down on paper. Then a thought pushes into my mind: Hide behind the desk. I'm not writing because I've got something important to think about. What's writing? Writing doesn't mean anything. We are absolved; the desk makes up for everything; it compensates. When my editor became convinced that all his efforts had been in vain and that there was no way to get me doing office work, he decided to do something with me. It would be best if I went somewhere. One day he summoned me to say there were some roubles in the office account and I should go write something. I got on a plane and flew beyond the Caucasus and then in the direction of Bukhara and points east. But that is a different world, not the world of this book.

High Time I Started Writing the
Next Unwritten Book . . .

. . . or rather its plan, or even disjointed fragments of a plan, because if it were a complete and finished work it would not fit into an existing book to which I have already added one non-existent book.

1

After returning from Central Asia, I stayed only briefly in Warsaw. In the autumn of that same year, 1967, I left for five years in Latin America. My first stop was Santiago de Chile, a bizarre architectural concoction built like a floating miniature Manhattan, a sea of town houses done in the perverse and capricious style of the Spanish secession—the luxurious and exclusive districts like Los Leones, Apoquindo and Vitacura—and then, on the outskirts, the endless wooden lean-tos known as *callampas*, full of the proletariat, the poor and all sorts of riff-raff. I had always taken the Chileans for peaceful people, easygoing and even effete (the city contains a multitude of cosmetics parlours for men, where gentlemen are given pedicures and have their nails painted), until suddenly, the day after the death of Salvador Allende, many of those nails turned out to be claws. Upon arriving in Santiago I went to a rental bureau where they gave me a map of the city and a list of suitable addresses. Then I began hunting down the houses and inspecting vacant lodgings. In this way I discovered a world I had never known existed. The owners of these furnished apartments were aged ladies, widows, divorcées and old maids in slippers, bonnets and furs. After greeting me, they would lead me around improbably cluttered rooms, then name some fantastic sum of money to be paid as rent, and finally bring out the lease which included not only the terms of the agreement but also a list of the contents of the apartment. This list was a book, a volume, which could serve as a fascinating psychological document about the madness to which people can be led by their avarice and the impulse to possess unneeded objects. The lists specified hundreds, no, thousands, of meaningless gadgets, figurines, kitties, coasters, wall hangings, pictures, vases, candleholders, birds made of glass, plush, brass, felt, plastic, marble, artificial silk, bark, wax, satin, lacquer, paper, nutshells, wicker, seashells, whalebone, of gee-gaws, thingamajigs, doodads and whatchamacallits. Every one of these apartments was carefully filled to the ceiling with an inventory of this junk, kneaded together, jammed into a vortex of knick-knacks and fiddle-faddle of which the ladies would say the most insignificant bauble was touching, beautiful and priceless. Later I figured out that there was an unceasing circulation of things of no use to anyone in these middle-class neighbourhoods; that on every occasion some thing of no use to anyone is given as a gift and custom enjoins that the gift be reciprocated in the form of some other thing of no use to anyone, which is then placed (laid, hung) beside the other things of no use to anyone. After years of giving and receiving (buying, winning) gifts each apartment thus turns into a great warehouse of things of no use to anyone. Later still it dawned on me that half the shops in these neighbourhoods deal exclusively in all sorts of trinkets, mascots and bric-à-brac, and that this is an excellent trade that brings in heaps of profits. After years among Africans whose only property is (in many cases) a wooden hoe and whose only food is a banana plucked off the branch, this absurd avalanche of possessions that came tumbling down upon me every time I opened a door crushed and discouraged me. I saved myself with the thought that this was all a false introduction to the world of Latin America, which had to be—I told myself—different.

2

In reality, however, the residences of these old ladies were simply a pathological and kitschy manifestation of Latin America—that is, the universal prevalence of the baroque: baroque not only as a style of aesthetics and thought, but also as a general commitment to excess and eclecticism. There is a lot of everything here and everything is exaggerated; everything wants to impose itself, shock, knock the beholder sideways. It is as if we had poor vision, weak hearing and an imperfect sense of smell; as if we would simply be incapable of noticing anything that presented itself in a moderate or modest form. If there is a jungle, it has to be enormous (the Amazon); if there are mountains, they have to be gigantic (the Andes); if there is a plain, it has to be endless (the Pampas); if there is a river, it has to be the biggest (the Amazon). People of every possible race and cast of complexion: white, red, black, yellow, metys, mulatto. All cultures: Indian, Anglo-Saxon, Spanish, Lusitanian, French, Hindu, Italian and African. Every possible and impossible political orientation and party. An excess of wealth and an excess of poverty. Gestures full of pathos and a flowery language with a multitude of adjectives. Market-places, bazaars, booths and displays piled high and straining under the weight of fruit, vegetables, flowers, clothes, cooking vessels, tools—all of it constantly multiplying itself, propagating under the ground, on the stones, on counters, in hands, in a hundred colours, its brightness and contrasts striking, exploding. This is not a world you can walk through with a calm head and an indifferent heart. You force your way through with difficulty, powerless and feeling as lost as when you look at a Diego Rivera fresco or read the prose of Lezama Lima. Fact is mixed with fantasy here, truth with myth, realism with rhetoric.

3

I spent a long time forcing my way through that underbrush, the exuberance, the façades and the repetitions, the ornamentation and the demagogy, before I reached the person, before I could feel at home among these people and recognize their dramas, their defeats, moods, romanticism, their honour and treason, their loneliness.

4

Describe the old Indian in the Mexican desert. I was driving along in a car and far off I spotted something that looked like an Indian hat lying on the sand. I stopped and walked towards it. Under the hat sat an Indian in a shallow hole that he had dug in the sand to protect himself from the wind. In front of him stood a wooden gramophone with a shabby, bashed-in megaphone. The old man was turning the crank the whole time (the wind-up spring was obviously long gone) and playing one record—he had only one record—which was so worn out that the grooves were barely there. From the tube issued a hoarse roar, crackling and the disordered tatters of a Latin American song: *Rio Manzanares dejame pasar* (Rio Manzanares, let me cross). Even though I had greeted him and stood in front of him for a long time, the old man paid no attention to me. 'Papa,' I finally shouted, 'there is no river here.'

He kept quiet. Then, after a while, he replied, 'Son, I am the river and I can't cross myself.' He said nothing more, but kept turning the crank and listening to the record.

5

Describe the story of the Bolivian army sergeant, Mario Terana, who shot the wounded Che Guevara dead. Two days later, he began to feel afraid. He stopped answering orders or questions. The army discharged him. To disguise himself he went around in dark glasses. Then he began to be afraid of the dark glasses, because he thought they would serve as a mark of recognition for the avengers of Guevara. He locked himself in his house and did not go outside for a long time. But then he began to fear his house, since it was like a trap where the partisans hunting him could easily lay hold of him. He stopped drinking, afraid that every liquid contained poison. He wandered off in an unknown direction for two days. On the evening of the second day he shot himself in the neighbourhood of the small, poor village of Madre de Dios.

6

About what happened to my friend Pedro Morote, a Peruvian. As a young boy Pedro declared war on the upper classes and fought in a partisan unit led by his friend, the poet Javier Heraud. In May 1963, they walked into an ambush in Puerto Maldonado and Heraud, then twenty-one, tried to escape across a river when he was shot dead by the police. Pedro managed to get away and went into hiding. When the army later seized power, times changed, and Pedro re-emerged in the struggle against the upper classes as an agricultural reform activist. We drove together to the most out-of-the-way Indian villages, where Pedro was distributing land to the poverty-stricken and benighted peasants. One day, on his return from one of these expeditions, Pedro learned that a friend of his had died and left him a considerable sum of money. In an instant everything changed. The partisan and reformer opened one of the most expensive and elegant nightspots in Lima, aimed at the upper-class market. Whoever turned up there—it was called *La Palisada*—could see a thick-set, stocky brown-haired man in a dinner jacket circulating among the tables, alert, contented (business was good) and accommodating. This was Pedro. He had put on a lot of weight, but he was brisk and strong. As he drifted through the room he was humming something under his breath. It is doubtful that any of the elegant clients knew that Pedro was singing the verses of his friend and leader Javier Heraud, who had died in an ambush so long ago.

7

Describe the market-place in the little town of Quetzaltepec (north of Oaxaca in Mexico). In the morning Indians of the Mixes tribe come in from the surrounding mountains. They arrive at the market carrying their wares on their backs, in bundles, in baskets. They spread everything out on the ground in the shade of the acacias planted around the large square. A kilogram of corn costs 1.25 pesos; beans 1.75 pesos; one hundred oranges two pesos; one hundred avocados three pesos. It is a silent market; nobody cries out his goods; transactions take place without words in an atmosphere characterized by the complete indifference of the buyer to the seller and the seller to the buyer. Around noon the heat sets in, the trading slows to a halt, then dies out and everybody gathers in the dark Indian bars (*puestos de mescal*) around the market-place. A litre of *mescal* costs four pesos. The business ends in the complete drunkenness of everybody who took part in the market. Afterwards the drunks—men, women and children—return to their villages running into each other, falling down in the sand or on the stones and picking themselves up, returning home without a centavo, fuddled and destitute.

8

Describe the soccer war.

THE SOCCER WAR

Luis Suarez said there was going to be a war, and I believed whatever Luis said. We were staying together in Mexico. Luis was giving me a lesson in Latin America: what it is and how to understand it. He could foresee many events. In his time he had predicted the fall of Goulart in Brazil, the fall of Bosch in the Dominican Republic and of Jimenez in Venezuela. Long before the return of Perón he believed that the old *caudillo* would again become president of Argentina; he foretold the sudden death of the Haitian dictator François Duvalier at a time when everybody said Papa Doc had many years left. Luis knew how to pick his way through Latin politics, in which amateurs like me got bogged down and blundered helplessly with each step.

This time Luis announced his belief that there would be a war after putting down the newspaper in which he had read a report on the soccer match between the Honduran and Salvadoran national teams. The two countries were playing for the right to take part in the 1970 World Cup in Mexico.

The first match was held on Sunday 8 June 1969, in the Honduran capital, Tegucigalpa.

Nobody in the world paid any attention.

The Salvadoran team arrived in Tegucigalpa on Saturday and spent a sleepless night in their hotel. The team could not sleep because it was the target of psychological warfare waged by the Honduran fans. A swarm of people encircled the hotel. The crowd threw stones at the windows and beat sheets of tin and empty barrels with sticks. They set off one string of firecrackers after another. They leaned on the horns of cars parked in front of the hotel. The fans whistled, screamed and sent up hostile chants. This went on all night. The idea was that a sleepy, edgy, exhausted team would be bound to lose. In Latin America these are common practices.

The next day Honduras defeated the sleepless El Salvador squad one-nil.

Eighteen-year-old Amelia Bolanios was sitting in front of the television in El Salvador when the Honduran striker Roberto Cardona scored the winning goal in the final minute. She got up and ran to the desk which contained her father's pistol in a drawer. She then shot herself in the heart. 'The young girl could not bear to see her fatherland brought to its knees,' wrote the Salvadoran newspaper *El Nacional* the next day. The whole capital took part in the televised funeral of Amelia Bolanios. An army honour guard marched with a flag at the head of the procession. The president of the republic and his ministers walked behind the flag-draped coffin. Behind the government came the Salvadoran soccer eleven who, booed, laughed at, and spat on at the Tegucigalpa airport, had returned to El Salvador on a special flight that morning.

But the return match of the series took place in San Salvador, the beautifully named Flor Blanca stadium, a week later. This time it was the Honduran team that spent a sleepless night. The screaming crowd of fans broke all the windows in the hotel and threw rotten eggs, dead rats and stinking rags inside. The players were taken to the match in armoured cars of the First Salvadoran Mechanized Division—which saved them from revenge and bloodshed at the hands of the mob that lined the route, holding up portraits of the national heroine Amelia Bolanios.

The army surrounded the ground. On the pitch stood a cordon of soldiers from a crack regiment of the *Guardia Nacional*, armed with sub-machine-guns. During the playing of the Honduran national anthem the crowd roared and whistled. Next, instead of the Honduran flag—which had been burnt before the eyes of the spectators, driving them mad with joy—the hosts ran a dirty, tattered dishrag up the flag-pole. Under such conditions the players from Tegucigalpa did not, understandably, have their minds on the game. They had their minds on getting out alive. 'We're awfully lucky that we lost,' said the visiting coach, Mario Griffin, with relief.

El Salvador prevailed, three-nil.

The same armoured cars carried the Honduran team straight from the playing field to the airport. A worse fate awaited the visiting fans. Kicked and beaten, they fled towards the border. Two of them died. Scores landed in hospital. One hundred and fifty of the visitors' cars were burned. The border between the two states was closed a few hours later.

Luis read about all of this in the newspaper and said that there was going to be a war. He had been a reporter for a long time and he knew his beat.

In Latin America, he said, the border between soccer and politics is vague. There is a long list of governments that have fallen or been overthrown after the defeat of the national team. Players on the losing team are denounced in the press as traitors. When Brazil won the World Cup in Mexico, an exiled Brazilian colleague of mine was heartbroken: 'The military right wing,' he said, 'can be assured of at least five more years of peaceful rule.' On the way to the title, Brazil beat England. In an article with the headline 'Jesus Defends Brazil', the Rio de Janeiro paper *Jornal dos Sportes* explained the victory thus: 'Whenever the ball flew towards our goal and a score seemed inevitable, Jesus reached his foot out of the clouds and cleared the ball.' Drawings accompanied the article, illustrating the supernatural intervention.

Anyone at the stadium can lose his life. Take the match that Mexico lost to Peru, two-one. An embittered Mexican fan shouted in an ironic tone, '*Viva* Mexico!' A moment

159

later he was dead, massacred by the crowd. But sometimes the heightened emotions find an outlet in other ways. After Mexico beat Belgium one-nil, Augusto Mariaga, the warden of a maximum-security prison in Chilpancingo (Guerrero State, Mexico), became delirious with joy and ran around firing a pistol into the air and shouting, '*Viva* Mexico!' He opened all the cells, releasing 142 dangerous hardened criminals. A court acquitted him later, as, according to the verdict, he had 'acted in patriotic exaltation.'

'Do you think it's worth going to Honduras?' I asked Luis, who was then editing the serious and influential weekly *Siempre*.

'I think it's worth it,' he answered. 'Something's bound to happen.'

I was in Tegucigalpa the next morning.

At dusk a plane flew over Tegucigalpa and dropped a bomb. Everybody heard it. The nearby mountains echoed its violent blast so that some said later that a whole series of bombs had been dropped. Panic swept the city. People fled home; merchants closed their shops. Cars were abandoned in the middle of the street. A woman ran along the pavement, crying, 'My child! My child!' Then silence fell and everything became still. It was as if the city had died. The lights went out and Tegucigalpa sank into darkness.

I hurried to the hotel, burst into my room, fed a piece of paper into the typewriter and tried to write a dispatch to Warsaw. I was trying to move fast because I knew that at that moment I was the only foreign correspondent there and that I could be the first to inform the world about the outbreak of the war in Central America. But it was pitch dark in the room and I couldn't see anything. I felt my way downstairs to the reception desk, where I was lent a candle. I went back upstairs, lit the candle and turned on my transistor radio. The announcer was reading a communiqué from the Honduran government about the commencement of hostilities with El Salvador. Then came the news that the Salvadoran army was attacking Honduras all along the front line.

I began to write:

TEGUCIGALPA (HONDURAS) PAP JULY 14 VIA TROPICAL RADIO RCA TODAY AT 6 PM WAR BEGAN BETWEEN EL SALVADOR AND HONDURAS SALVADORAN AIR FORCE BOMBARDED FOUR HONDURAN CITIES STOP AT SAME TIME SALVADORAN ARMY CROSSED HONDURAN BORDER ATTEMPTING TO PENETRATE DEEP INTO COUNTRY STOP IN RESPONSE TO AGGRESSION HONDURAN AIR FORCE BOMBARDED IMPORTANT SALVADORAN INDUSTRIAL AND STRATEGIC TARGETS AND GROUND FORCES BEGAN DEFENSIVE ACTION

At this moment someone in the street started shouting '*Apaga la luz!*' ('Turn off the light!') over and over, more and more loudly with increasing agitation. I blew out the candle. I went on typing blind, by touch, striking a match over the keys every now and then.

RADIO REPORTS FIGHTING UNDERWAY ALONG FULL LENGTH OF FRONT AND THAT HONDURAN ARMY IS INFLICTING HEAVY LOSSES ON SALVADORAN ARMY STOP GOVERNMENT HAS CALLED WHOLE POPULATION TO DEFENCE OF ENDANGERED NATION AND APPEALED TO UN FOR CONDEMNATION OF ATTACK

I carried the dispatch downstairs, found the owner of the hotel and began asking him to find someone to lead me to the post office. It was my first day there and I did not know Tegucigalpa at all. It is not a big city—a quarter of a million people—but it lies among hills and has a maze of crabbed streets. The owner wanted to help but he had no one to send with me and I was in a hurry. In the end he called the police. Nobody at the police station had time. So he called the fire department. Three firemen arrived in full gear, wearing helmets and carrying axes. We greeted each other in the dark; I could not see their faces. I begged them to lead me to the post office. I know Honduras well, I lied, and know that its people are renowned for their hospitality. I was sure they would not refuse me. It was very important that the world find out the truth about who started the war, who shot first and I could assure them that I had written the honest truth. The main thing now was time, and we had to hurry.

We left the hotel. It was a dark night. I could see only the outlines of the street. I do not know why we spoke in whispers. I tried to remember the way and counted my steps. I was close to a thousand when the firemen stopped and one of them knocked on a door. A voice from inside asked what we wanted. Then the door opened, but only for an instant so that the light wouldn't be seen. I was inside. They ordered me to wait: there is only one telex machine in Honduras, and the president was using it. He was engaged in an exchange with his ambassador in Washington, who would be applying to the American government for military assistance. This went on for a long time, since the president and the ambassador were using uncommonly flowery language and, besides, the connection kept breaking every so often.

After midnight I finally made contact with Warsaw. The machine typed out the number TL 813480 PAP VARSOVIA. I leapt up joyfully. The operator asked, 'Is Varsovia some country?'

'It's not a country. It's a city. The country is called *Polonia.*'

'*Polonia, Polonia,*' he repeated, but I could see that the name didn't actually interest him.

He asked Warsaw, 'HOW RECEIVED MSG BIBI?'

And Warsaw answered, 'RECEIVED OK OK GREE FOR RYSIEK TKS TKS!'

I put my arms around the operator, told him I hoped he got through the war in one piece and started back to the hotel. Barely had I set foot in the street when I realized I was lost. I found myself in terrible darkness—thick and clotted and impenetrable, as if a heavy black grease had been smeared over my eyes, and I could see nothing, not even, literally, my hands when I stretched them out in front of me. The sky must have clouded over, because the stars had disappeared and there was no light anywhere. I was alone in an unfamiliar city that, as I couldn't see it, might well have disappeared into the earth. The silence was piercing—not a voice anywhere, not a sound. I moved forward like a blind man, feeling the walls, the drainpipes and the mesh shutters over the shop windows. When I realized that my footsteps were sounding like drumbeats I went up on tiptoe. Suddenly the wall at my fingertips ended; I would have to turn into a side street. Or was it the beginning of a plaza? Or was I on a high escarpment with a long drop in front of me? I tested the ground ahead with my feet. Asphalt! I was in the middle of the street. I moved sideways and bumped into another wall. I no longer knew where the post office could be, let alone the hotel; I was floundering, but I kept going. Suddenly there was a powerful boom! I was losing my footing and was being thrown to the pavement.

I had upset a tin garbage can.

The street must have been on a slope, because the

garbage can rolled away with a frightful din. In an instant I heard windows snapping open on all sides above me and hysterical, terrified whispers: 'Silencio! Silencio!' A city that wanted the world to forget it for one night, that wanted to be alone in silence and darkness, was defending itself against being given away. As the empty garbage can clattered down the hill, more and more windows kept opening as it passed with plaintive, insistent whispers: 'Silencio! Silencio!' But there was no way to stop the metal monster, it was like something possessed, banging against the cobblestones, smashing into lamp-posts, thundering and booming. I lay on the pavement, hugging it, frightened, sweating. I was afraid that someone would open fire in my direction. I had committed an act of treason: the enemy, unable to find the city in this darkness and silence, could now locate it by the racket of the garbage can. I had to make tracks and run. I got to my feet and found that my head was throbbing—I had struck it on the pavement when I fell—and I sprinted like a madman until I stumbled over something and fell on my face, the taste of blood in my mouth. I picked myself up and leaned against a wall. The wall arched above my head and I had to stand hunched over, feeling more and more imprisoned by a city I could not see. I watched for the light of a lantern: somebody must be looking for me, this intruder who had violated the military order not to go out at night. But there was nothing, only sepulchral silence and unviolated darkness. I crept along with my hands stretched out in front of me, bruised now and bleeding and bloody in a tattered shirt, lost in this labyrinth of walls. Centuries could have passed; I might have reached the end of the world. Suddenly a violent tropical deluge broke. Lightning illuminated the nightmare city for an instant. Standing among unknown streets I glimpsed a decrepit townhouse, a wooden shed, a street-lamp, cobble-stones. It vanished in a second. I could hear only the gush of rain and, from time to time, the whistle of wind. I was freezing, soaked, shivering all over. I felt the recess of a doorway and took cover from the downpour. Jammed between the wall and the door I tried to sleep, but without success.

An army patrol found me at dawn.

'Silly man,' a sleepy sergeant said. 'Where were you strolling on a wartime evening?' He looked me over suspiciously and wanted to take me to city headquarters. Fortunately I was carrying my papers and managed to explain what had happened. They led me to my hotel and on the way mentioned that the battle at the front had gone on all night, but that it was so far away that you couldn't hear the shooting in Tegucigalpa.

Since early morning people had been digging trenches, erecting barricades—preparing for a siege. Women were stocking up supplies and criss-crossing their windows with masking tape. People rushed through the streets directionless; an atmosphere of panic reigned. Student brigades were painting outsized slogans on walls and fences. A bubble full of graffiti had burst over Tegucigalpa, covering the walls with thousands of verses.

ONLY AN IMBECILE WORRIES
NOBODY BEATS HONDURAS

or:

PICK UP YOUR GUNS AND LET'S GO GUYS
CUT THOSE SALVADORANS DOWN TO SIZE

WE SHALL AVENGE THREE-NIL

PORFIRIO RAMOS SHOULD BE ASHAMED OF HIMSELF FOR
LIVING WITH A SALVADORAN WOMAN

ANYONE SEEING RAIMUNDO GRANADOS CALL THE POLICE
HE'S A SALVADORAN SPY

Latins are obsessed with spies, intelligence conspiracies
and plots. In war, everyone is a fifth-columnist. I was not in
a particularly comfortable situation: official propaganda on
both sides blamed communists for every misfortune, and I
was the only correspondent in the region from a socialist
country. Even so, I wanted to see the war through to the
end.

I went to the post office and asked the telex operator
to join me for a beer. He was terrified, because, although
he had a Honduran father, his mother was a citizen of
El Salvador. He was a mixed national and thus among
the suspects. He did not know what would happen next.
All morning the police had been herding Salvadorans
into provisional camps, most often set up in stadiums.
Throughout Latin America, stadiums play a double role: in
peacetime they are sports venues; in war they turn into
concentration camps.

His name was José Malaga, and we had a drink in a
restaurant near the post office. Our uncertain status had
made brothers of us. Every so often José phoned his
mother, who was sitting locked in her house, and said,
'Mama, everything's OK. They haven't come for me; I'm
still working.'

By the afternoon the other correspondents arrived from
Mexico, forty of them, my colleagues. They had flown into
Guatemala and then hired a bus, because the airport in
Tegucigalpa was closed. They all wanted to drive to the
front. We went to the Presidential Palace, an ugly, bright
blue turn-of-the-century building in the centre of the town,

to arrange permission. There were machine-gun nests and sandbags around the palace, and anti-aircraft guns in the courtyard. In the corridors inside, soldiers were dozing or lolling around in full battledress.

People have been making war for thousands of years, but each time it is as if it is the first war ever waged, as if everyone has started from scratch.

A captain appeared and said he was the army press spokesman. He was asked to describe the situation and he stated that they were winning all along the front and that the enemy was suffering heavy casualties.

'OK,' said the AP correspondent. 'Let's see the front.'

The Americans, the captain explained, were already there. They always go first because of their influence—and because they commanded obedience and could arrange all sorts of things. The captain said we could go the next day, and that everyone should bring two photographs.

We drove to a place where two artillery pieces stood under some trees. Cannons were firing and stacks of ordnance were lying around. Ahead of us we could see the road that led to El Salvador. Swamp stretched along both sides of the road, and dense green bush began past the belt of swamp.

The sweaty, unshaven major charged with holding the road said we could go no further. Beyond this point both armies were in action, and it was hard to tell who was who or what belonged to which side. The bush was too thick to see anything. Two opposing units often noticed each other only at the last moment, when, wandering through the overgrowth, they met face to face. In addition, since both armies wore the same uniforms, carried the same equipment, and spoke the same language, it was difficult to distinguish friend from foe.

The major advised us to return to Tegucigalpa, because

advancing might mean getting killed without even knowing who had done it. (As if that mattered, I thought.) But the television cameramen said they had to push forward, to the front line, to film soldiers in action, firing, dying. Gregor Straub of NBC said he had to have a close-up of a soldier's face dripping sweat. Rodolfo Carillo of CBS said he had to catch a despondent commander sitting under a bush and weeping because he had lost his whole unit. A French cameraman wanted a panorama shot with a Salvadoran unit charging a Honduran unit from one side, or vice versa. Somebody else wanted to capture the image of a soldier carrying his dead comrade. The radio reporters sided with the cameramen. One wanted to record the cries of a casualty summoning help, growing weaker and weaker, until he breathed his last breath. Charles Meadows of Radio Canada wanted the voice of a soldier cursing war amid a hellish racket of gunfire. Naotake Mochida of Radio Japan wanted the bark of an officer shouting to his commander over the roar of artillery—using a Japanese field telephone.

Many others also decided to go forward. Competition is a powerful incentive. Since American television was going, the American wire services had to go as well. Since the Americans were going, Reuters had to go. Excited by patriotic ambition, I decided, as the only Pole on the scene, to attach myself to the group that intended to make the desperate march. Those who said they had bad hearts, or professed to be uninterested in particulars since they were writing general commentaries, we left behind, under a tree.

There might have been twenty of us who set out along an empty road bathed in intense sunlight. The risk, or even the madness, of the march lay in the fact that the road ran along the top of an embankment: we were perfectly visible to both of the armies hiding in the bush that began about a hundred yards away. One good burst of machine-gun fire in our direction would be enough.

At the beginning everything went well. We heard intense gunfire and the detonation of artillery shells but it was a mile or so away. To keep our spirits up we were all talking (nervously and without necessarily making sense). But soon fear began to take its toll. It is, indeed, a rather unpleasant feeling to walk with the awareness that at any moment a bullet can find you. No one, however, acknowledged fear openly. First, somebody simply proposed we take a rest. So we sat down and caught our breath. Then, when we started again, two began lagging behind—apparently. immersed in conversation. Then somebody spotted an especially interesting group of trees that deserved long, careful inspection. Then two others announced that they had to go back because they had forgotten the filters they needed for their cameras. We took another rest. We rested more and more often, and the pauses grew longer. There were ten of us left.

In the meantime, nothing was happening in our vicinity. We were walking along an empty road in the direction of El Salvador. The air was wonderful. The sun was setting. That very sun helped us extricate ourselves. The television men suddenly pulled out their light metres and declared that it was already too dark to film. Nothing could be done—not long shots, or close-ups, or action-shots, or stills. And it was a long way to the front line yet. By the time we got there it would be night.

The whole group started back. The ones who had heart trouble, who were going to write general commentaries, who had turned back earlier because they had been talking or had forgotten their filters, were waiting for us under the tree beside the two artillery pieces.

The sweaty, unshaven major had organized an army truck

to carry us to our billets for the night, at a village behind the line called Nacaome. There we held a conference and decided that the Americans would phone the president immediately to request an order for us to see the whole front, to have us transported into the very midst of the fighting, into the hell of gunfire, on to ground soaked with blood.

In the morning an airplane arrived to take us to the far end of the front, where heavy fighting was in progress. Overnight rain had turned the grass airstrip at Nacaome into a quagmire, and the dilapidated old DC-3, black with exhaust smoke, stuck up out of the water like a hydroplane. It had been shot up the day before by a Salvadoran fighter; the holes in its fuselage were patched with rough boards. The sight of these ordinary, simple boards of wood frightened those who said they had bad hearts. They stayed behind and returned later to Tegucigalpa.

We were to fly to Santa Rosa de Copán at the other extreme of the front. As it was taking off the plane trailed as much smoke and flame as a rocket starting for the moon. In the air it screeched and groaned and reeled like a drunk swept along in an autumn gale. It plunged maniacally earthwards and then clambered desperately for altitude. Never level, never in a straight line. The cabin—the plane usually carried freight—contained no seats or benches of any kind. We gripped curved metal handholds to avoid being thrown against the walls. The wind blowing in through the gaping holes was enough to tear our heads off. The two pilots, carefree youngsters, grinned at us the whole time in the cockpit mirror as if they enjoyed some private joke.

'The main thing,' Antonio Rodriguez of the Spanish news agency EFE hollered to me over the roar of the propellors and the wind, 'is for the motors to hold out. *Mama mia*, let the motors hold out!'

In Santa Rosa de Copán, a sleepy hamlet filled then only with soldiers, a truck carried us through muddy streets to the barracks, which stood in the old Spanish fort, surrounded by a grey wall swollen from the damp. Once inside we heard three wounded prisoners in the courtyard.

'Talk!' the interrogating officer was shouting at them. 'Tell me everything!'

The prisoners mumbled. They were stripped to the waist and weak from loss of blood—the first with a belly wound, the second with one to his shoulder, the third with part of his hand shot away. The one with the belly wound didn't last long. He groaned, turned as if it were a step in a dance and fell to the ground. The remaining two went silent and looked at their colleague with the flat gaze of landed fish.

An officer led us to the garrison commander who, pale and tired, did not know what to do with us. He ordered that military shirts be given to us. He ordered his aide to bring coffee. The commander was worried that Salvadoran units might arrive any moment. Santa Rosa lay along the enemy's main line of attack—that is, along the road that connected the Atlantic and the Pacific. El Salvador, lying on the Pacific, dreamed of conquering Honduras, lying on the Atlantic. In this way little El Salvador would become a two-ocean power. The shortest path from El Salvador to the Atlantic ran right where we were—through Ocotepeque, Santa Rosa de Copán, San Pedro Sula, to Puerto Cortés. Advancing Salvadoran tanks had already penetrated deep into Honduran territory. The Salvadorans were moving to order: push through to the Atlantic, then to Europe and then the world!

Their radio repeated: 'A little shouting and noise and that's the end of Honduras.'

Weaker and poorer, Honduras was defending itself fiercely. Through the open barracks window we could see the higher-ranking officers preparing their units for the front. Young conscripts stood in scraggly ranks. They were small dark boys, Indians all, with tense faces, terrified—but ready to fight. The officers said something and pointed at the distant horizon. Afterwards a priest appeared and sprinkled holy water on platoons going out towards death.

In the afternoon we left for the front in an open truck. The first forty kilometres passed without incident. The road led through higher and higher country, among green heights covered with thick tropical bush. Empty clay huts, some of them burnt out, clung to the mountain slopes. In one place we passed the inhabitants of an entire village straggling along the edge of the road, carrying bundles. Later, as we drove past, a crowd of peasants in white shirts and sombreros flourished their machetes and shotguns. Artillery fire could be heard far, far away.

Suddenly there was a commotion in the road. We had reached a triangular clearing in the forest where the casualties had been brought. Some were lying on stretchers, and others right on the grass. A few soldiers and two orderlies moved among them. There was no doctor. Four soldiers were digging a hole nearby. The wounded lay there calmly, patiently, and the most amazing thing was patience, the unimaginable superhuman endurance of pain. No one was crying out, no one was calling for help. The soldiers brought them water and the orderlies applied primitive dressings as well as they could. What I saw there staggered me. One of the orderlies, with a lancet in his hand, was going from one casualty to another and digging the bullets out of them, as if he were paring the core out of an apple. The other orderly poured iodine on the wounds and then pressed on the bandage.

A wounded boy arrived in a truck. A Salvadoran. He had

taken a bullet in the knee. He was ordered to lie down on the grass. The boy was barefoot, pale, spattered with blood. The orderly poked around in his knee, looking for the bullet. The boy moaned.

'Quiet, you poor bastard,' the orderly said. 'You're distracting me.'

He used his fingers to pull out the bullet. Then he poured iodine into the wound and wrapped it in a bandage.

'Stand up and go to the truck,' said a soldier from the escort.

The boy picked himself up off the the grass and hobbled to the vehicle. He didn't say a word, didn't make a sound.

'Climb in,' the soldier commanded. We rushed to give the boy a hand, but the soldier waved us away with his rifle. Something was bothering the soldier; he'd been at the front; his nerves were jangly. The boy rested himself on the high tailgate and dragged himself in. His body hit the bed of the truck with a thud. I thought he was finished. But a moment later his grey, naive, quizzical face appeared, waiting humbly for the next stroke of destiny.

'How about a smoke?' he asked us in a quiet, hoarse voice. We tossed whatever cigarettes we had into the truck. The vehicle moved off, and the boy was grinning at having enough cigarettes to share with his whole village.

The orderlies were giving glucose intravenously to a dying soldier, who had drawn many interested onlookers. Some were sitting around the stretcher where he was lying, and others were leaning on their rifles. He might have been, say, twenty. He had taken eleven rounds. An older, weaker man hit by those eleven rounds would have been dead long ago. But the bullets had ripped into a young body, strong and powerfully built, and death was meeting resistance. The wounded man lay unconscious, already on the other side of existence, but some remnant of life was putting up a last desperate fight. The soldier was stripped to the waist, and everyone could see his muscles contracting and the sweat beading up on his sallow skin. The tense muscles and streams of sweat showed the ferocity of battle, when life goes against death. Everybody was interested in it because everybody wanted to know how much strength there was in life and how much there was in death. Everybody wanted to see how long life could hold off death and whether a young life that's still there and doesn't want to give up would be able to outlast death.

'Maybe he'll make it,' one of the soldiers ventured.

'No way,' the orderly replied, holding the bottle of glucose at arm's length above the casualty.

There was a gloomy silence. The casualty inhaled violently, as if he had just finished a long hard run.

'Doesn't anybody know him?' one of the soldiers asked eventually.

The wounded man's heart was working at maximum effort; we felt its feverish thumping.

'Nobody,' another soldier answered.

A truck was climbing the road, its motor complaining. Four soldiers were digging a hole down in the woods.

'Is he ours or theirs?' a soldier sitting by the stretcher asked.

'Nobody knows,' said the orderly after a moment's quiet.

'He's his mother's,' a soldier standing nearby said.

'He's God's now,' added another after a pause. He took off his cap and hung it on the barrel of the rifle.

The casualty shivered, and his muscles pulsed under his glossy yellowish skin.

'Life is so strong,' a soldier leaning on his rifle said in astonishment. 'It's still there, still there.'

Everyone was absorbed, silent, concentrating on the sight of the wounded man. He was drawing breath more slowly now, and his head had tilted back. The soldiers sitting near him grasped their hands around their knees and hunched up, as if the fire was burning low and the cold creeping in. In the end—it was a while yet—somebody said: 'He's gone. All he was is gone.'

They stayed there for some time, looking fearfully at the dead man and afterwards, when they saw that nothing else would happen, they began walking away.

We drove on. The road snaked through forested mountains, past the village of San Francisco. A series of curves began, one after another, and suddenly around one curve we ran into the maw of the war. Soldiers were running and firing, bullets whizzed overhead, long bursts of machine-gun fire ripped along both sides of the road. The driver braked suddenly and at that instant a shell exploded in front of us. Sweet Jesus, I thought, this is it. What felt like the wing of a typhoon swept through the truck. Everybody dived for it, one on top of another, just to make it to the ground, to hit the ditch, to vanish. Out of the corner of my eye, on the run, I could see the fat French TV cameraman scrambling along the road looking for his equipment. Somebody shouted, 'Take cover!' and when he heard that order—grenades going off and the bark of automatic rifles hadn't fazed him—he hugged the road like a dead man.

I lunged in the direction that seemed to be the most quiet, threw myself into the bushes, down, down, as far as I could get from the curve where the shell had hit us, downhill, along bare ground, skating across slick clay, and then into the bush, deep into the bush, but I didn't run far because suddenly there was shooting right in front of me—bullets flying around, branches fluttering, a machine-gun roaring. I fell and crouched on the ground.

When I opened my eyes I saw a piece of soil and ants crawling over it.

They were walking along their paths, one after another,

in various directions. It wasn't the time for observing ants, but the very sight of them marching along, the sight of another world, another reality, brought me back to consciousness. An idea came into my head: if I could control my fear enough to stop my ears for a moment and look only at these insects, I could begin to think with some sort of sense. I lay among the thick bushes plugging my ears with all my might, nose in the dirt and I watched the ants.

I don't know how long this went on. When I raised my head, I was looking into the eyes of a soldier.

I froze. Falling into the hands of the Salvadorans was what I feared most, because then the only thing to look forward to was certain death. They were a brutal army, blind with fury, shooting whomever they got hold of in the madness of the war. In any case, this was what I thought, having been fed Honduran propaganda. An American or an Englishman might have a chance, although not necessarily. In Nacaome the day before we had been shown an American missionary killed by the Salvadorans. And El Salvador did not even maintain diplomatic relations with Poland, so I would count for nothing.

The soldier was taken by surprise, too. Crawling through the bush, he hadn't noticed me until the last moment. He adjusted his helmet, which was adorned with grass and leaves. He had a dark, skinny, furrowed face. In his hands there was an old Mauser.

'Who are you?' he asked.

'And what army are you from?'

'Honduras,' he said, because he could tell right off that I was a foreigner, neither his nor theirs.

'Honduras! Dear brother!' I rejoiced and pulled the piece of paper out of my pocket. It was the document from the Honduran high command, from Colonel Ramirez Ortega, to the units at the front permitting me to enter the region of military activity. Each of us had been given the same document in Tegucigalpa before leaving for the front.

I told the soldier that I had to get to Santa Rosa and then to Tegucigalpa so that I could send a dispatch to Warsaw. The soldier was happy because he was already calculating that with an order from the general staff (the documents commanded all subordinates to assist me) he could withdraw to the rear along with me.

'We will go together, *señor*,' the soldier said. '*Señor* will say that he has commanded me to accompany him.'

He was a recruit, a dirt farmer; he had been called up a week ago, he didn't know the army; the war meant nothing to him. He was trying to figure out how to survive it.

Shells were slamming around us. Far, far away we could hear shooting. Cannons were firing. The smell of powder and smoke was in the air. There were machine-guns behind us and on both sides.

His company had been crawling forward among the bushes, up this hill, when our truck came around the corner and drove into the turmoil of war and was abandoned. From where we lay pressing against the ground we could see the thick-ribbed gum soles of his company, only their soles, as the men crawled through the grass. Then the soles of their boots stopped, then they moved ahead, one-two, one-two, a few metres forward, and then they stopped again.

The soldier nudged me: '*Señor, mire cuantos zapatos!*' ('Look at all those shoes!')

He kept looking at the shoes of the other members of his company as they crawled forward. He blinked, weighed something in his mind and at last said hopelessly, '*Toda mi familia anda descalzada.*' ('My whole family goes barefoot.')

We started crawling through the forest.

177

The shooting let up for a moment and the soldier, fatigued, stopped. In a hushed voice he told me to wait where I was because he was going back to where his company had been fighting. He said that the living had certainly moved forward—their orders were to pursue the enemy to the very border—but the dead would remain on the battlefield and, for them, their boots were now superfluous. He would strip a few of the dead of their boots, hide them under a bush and mark the place. When the war was over, he would return and have enough boots for his whole family. He had already calculated that he could trade one pair of army boots for three pairs of children's shoes, and there were nine little ones back home.

It crossed my mind that he was going mad, so I told him that I was putting him under my orders and that we should keep crawling. But the soldier did not want to listen. He was driven by thoughts of footwear and he would throw himself into the front line in order to secure the property lying there in the grass, rather than let it be buried with the dead. Now the war had meaning for him, a point of reference and a goal. He knew what he wanted and what he had to do. I was certain that if he left me we would be separated and never meet again. The last thing I wanted was to be left alone in that forest: I did not know who controlled it or which army was where or which direction I should set off in. There is nothing worse than finding yourself alone in somebody else's country during somebody else's war. So I crawled after the soldier towards the battlefield. We crept to where the forest stopped and a new scene of combat could be observed through the stumps and bushes. The front had moved off laterally now: shells were bursting behind an elevation that rose up to the left of us, and somewhere to the right—underground, it seemed, but it must have been in a ravine—machine-guns were muttering.

An abandoned mortar stood in front of us, and in the grass lay dead soldiers.

I told my companion that I was going no further. He could do what he had to do, as long as he didn't get lost and returned quickly. He left his rifle with me and bolted ahead. I was so worried that someone would catch us there or pop up from behind the bushes or throw a grenade that I couldn't watch him. I felt sick lying there with my head on the wet dirt, smelling of rot and smoke. If only we don't get encircled, I thought, if only we can crawl closer to a peaceful world. This soldier of mine, I thought, is satisfied now. The clouds have parted above his head and the heavens are raining manna—he will return to the village, dump a sackful of boots on the floor and watch his children jump for joy.

The soldier came back dragging his conquest and hid it in the bushes. He wiped the sweat off his face and looked around to fix the spot in his mind. We moved back into the depth of the forest. It was drizzling and fog lay in the clearing. We walked in no specific direction but kept as far as possible from the commotion of the war. Somewhere, not far from there, must have been Guatemala. And further, Mexico. And further still, the United States. But for us at that moment, all those countries were on another planet. The inhabitants there had their own lives and thought about entirely different problems. Perhaps they did not know that we had a war here. No war can be conveyed over a distance. Somebody sits eating dinner and watching television: pillars of earth blown into the air; *cut*—the tracks of a charging tank; *cut*—soldiers falling and writhing in pain;—and the man watching television gets angry and curses because while he was gaping at the screen he oversalted his soup. War becomes a spectacle, a show, when it is seen from a distance and expertly re-shaped in the cutting room. In reality a soldier sees no further than his own nose, has his eyes full of sand or sweat, shoots at random and clings to the ground like a mole. Above all, he is frightened. The front line soldier says little: if questioned he might not answer at all, or might respond only by shrugging his shoulders. As a rule he walks around hungry and sleepy, not knowing what the next order will be or what will become of him in an hour. War makes for a constant familiarity with death and the experience of it sinks deep into the memory. Afterwards, in old age, a man reaches back more and more to his war memories, as if recollections of the front expand with time, as if he had spent his whole life in a foxhole.

Stealing through the forest, I asked the soldier why they were fighting with El Salvador. He replied that he did not know, that it was a government affair. I asked him how he could fight when he did not know why he was spilling blood. He answered that when you live in a village it's better not to ask questions because questions arouse the suspicions of the village mayor, and then the mayor would volunteer him for the road gang, and, on the road gang, he would have to neglect his farm and his family, and then the hunger waiting for him on his return would be even greater. And isn't the everyday poverty enough as it is? A man has to live in such a way that his name never reaches the ears of authorities. If it does, they write it down immediately and then that man is in for a lot of trouble later. Government matters are not fit for the mind of a village farmer, because the government understands such things but nobody's going to let a dirt farmer do anything.

Walking through the woods at sunset and straightening our backs because it was getting quieter all the time, we hit a small village plastered together out of clay and straw: Santa Teresa. An infantry battalion, decimated in the all-day battle, was billeted there. Exhausted and stunned by the experience of the front line, soldiers wandered among the huts. It was drizzling continuously and everybody was dirty, smeared with clay.

The people at the guardpost led us to the battalion commander. I showed him my documents and asked for transportation to Tegucigalpa. That worthy man offered me a car but ordered me to stay put until morning because the roads were soaked and mountainous and ran along the edges of cliffs, and at night, without lights, would be impassable. The commander sat in an abandoned hut listening to the radio. The announcer was reading a string of communiqués from the front. Next we heard that a wide range of governments, the countries of Latin America, along with many from Europe and Asia, wanted to bring the war between Honduras and El Salvador to an end, and had already issued statements about it. The African countries were expected to take a stand presently. Communiqués from Australia and Oceania were also expected. China was silent, which was provoking interest, and so, too, was Canada. The Canadian reticence could be explained by the fact that a Canadian correspondent, Charles Meadows, was at the front and his situation might be complicated or made more dangerous by a statement now.

The presenter then read that the Apollo 11 rocket had been launched from Cape Kennedy. Three astronauts, Armstrong, Aldrin and Collins, were flying to the moon. Man was drawing closer to the stars, opening new worlds, soaring into the infinite galaxies. Congratulations were pouring into Houston from all corners of the world, the presenter informed us, and all humanity was rejoicing at the triumph of reason and precise thinking.

My soldier was dozing in a corner. At dawn I woke him

up and said we were leaving. An exhausted battalion driver, still half-asleep, took us to Tegucigalpa in a jeep. To save time, we drove straight to the post office, where, on a borrowed typewriter, I wrote the dispatch that was later printed in the newspapers at home. José Malaga let the dispatch go out before all the others waiting to be sent and released it without the approval of the military censors (it was, after all, written in Polish).

My colleagues were returning from the front. They arrived one by one, because everyone had got lost after we drove into the artillery fire at that turning in the road. Enrique Amado had run into a Salvadoran patrol, three members of the *Guardia Rural*, the private *gendarmerie* maintained by the Salvadoran *latifundistas* and recruited from among the criminal element. Very dangerous types. They ordered Enrique to stand up to be executed. He played for time, praying at great length and then asking to be allowed to relieve himself. The *guardistas* obviously loved the sight of a man in terror. In the end they ordered him to make his final preparations and were taking aim when a series of shots rang out from the bushes. One of the patrol fell, hit, and the other two were taken prisoner.

The soccer war lasted one hundred hours. Its victims: 6,000 dead, more than 12,000 wounded. Fifty thousand people lost their homes and fields. Many villages were destroyed.

The two countries ceased military action because Latin American states intervened, but to this day there are exchanges of gunfire along the Honduras–El Salvador border, and people die, and villages are burned.

These are the real reasons for the war: El Salvador, the smallest country in Central America, has the greatest population density in the western hemisphere (over 160 people per square kilometre). Things are crowded, and all the more so because most of the land is in the hands of fourteen great landowning clans. People even say that El Salvador is the property of fourteen families. A thousand *latifundistas* own exactly ten times as much land as their hundred thousand peasants. Two thirds of the village population owns no land. For years a part of the landless poor has been emigrating to Honduras, where there are large tracts of unimproved land. Honduras (12,000 square kilometres) is almost six times as large as El Salvador, but has about half as many people (2,500,000). This was illegal emigration but was kept hushed-up, tolerated by the Honduran government for years.

Salvadoran peasants settled in Honduras, established villages, and grew accustomed to a better life than the one they had left behind. They numbered about 300,000.

In the 1960s, unrest began among the Honduran peasantry, which was demanding land, and the Honduras government passed a decree on agricultural reform. But since this was an oligarchical government, dependent on the United States, the decree did not break up the land of either the oligarchy or the large banana plantations belonging to the United Fruit Company. The government wanted to re-distribute the land occupied by the Salvadoran squatters, meaning that the 300,000 Salvadorans would have to return to their own country, where they had nothing, and where, in any event, they would be refused by the Salvadoran government, fearing a peasant revolution.

Relations between the two countries were tense. Newspapers on both sides waged a campaign of hate, slander and abuse, calling each other Nazis, dwarfs, drunkards, sadists, spiders, aggressors and thieves. There were pogroms. Shops were burned.

In these circumstances the match between Honduras and El Salvador had taken place.

The war ended in a stalemate. The border remained the same. It is a border established by sight in the bush, in mountainous terrain that both sides claim. Some of the émigrés returned to El Salvador and some of them are still living in Honduras. And both governments are satisfied: for several days Honduras and El Salvador occupied the front pages of the world press and were the object of interest and concern. The only chance small countries from the Third World have of evoking a lively international interest is when they decide to shed blood. This is a sad truth, but so it is.

The deciding game of the best-of-three series was held on neutral ground, in Mexico (El Salvador won, three-two). The Honduran fans were placed on one side of the stadium, the Salvadoran fans on the other side, and down the middle sat 5,000 Mexican police armed with thick clubs.

VICTORIANO GOMEZ ON TV

Victoriano Gomez died on 8 February in the small town of San Miguel, El Salvador. He was shot under the afternoon sun, in the football stadium. People had been sitting in the grandstand of the stadium since morning. Television and radio vans had arrived. The cameramen set up. Some press photographers stood on the green playing field, grouped around one of the goals. It looked as if a match was about to begin.

His mother was brought out first. The worn out, modestly dressed woman sat facing the place where her son was to die, and the people in the grandstand fell silent. But after a while, they began talking again, swapping comments, buying ice cream and cold drinks. The children made most of the noise. Those who could not find seats in the grandstand climbed a nearby tree for the view.

An army truck drove on to the field. First, the soldiers who would be in the firing squad got out. Victoriano Gomez jumped down lightly on to the grass after them. He looked around the grandstand, and said loudly, so loudly that many people heard him:'I am innocent, my friends.'

The stadium became quiet again, although whistles of disapproval could be heard from the places of honour where the local dignitaries sat.

The cameras went into action: the transmission was due to begin. All over El Salvador, people were watching the execution of Victoriano Gomez on television.

Victoriano stood near the running track, facing the grandstand. But the cameramen shouted at him to go to the middle of the stadium, so that they could have better light and a better picture. He understood and walked back into the middle of the field where he stood at attention—swarthy, tall, twenty-four years old. Now only a small figure could be seen from the grandstand and that was good. Death loses its literalness at that distance: it stops being death and instead becomes the spectacle of death. The cameramen had Victoriano in close-up, however; they had his face filling the screen; people watching television saw more than the crowd gathered in the stadium.

After the firing squad's volley, Victoriano fell and the cameras showed the soldiers surround his body to count the hits. They counted thirteen. The leader of the squad nodded and slid his pistol into his holster.

It was all over. The grandstand began to empty. The transmission came to an end. Victoriano and the soldiers left in the truck. His mother stayed a while longer, not moving, surrounded by a group of curious people who stared at her in silence.

I do not know what to add. Victoriano was a guerrilla in the San Miguel forests. He was a Salvadoran Robin Hood. He urged the peasants to seize land. All of El Salvador is the property of fourteen *latifundista* families. A million landless peasants live there too. Victoriano organized ambushes of *Guardia Rural* patrols. The *Guardia* is the *latifundistas'* private army, recruited from criminal elements, and the terror of every village. Victoriano declared war on these people.

The police caught him when he came to San Miguel at night to visit his mother. The news was celebrated on every hacienda. Unending fiestas were organized. The police chief was promoted and received congratulations from the president.

Victoriano was sentenced to death.

The government decided to promote his death. There are many dissatisfied, mutinous people in El Salvador. The peasants are demanding land and the students are crying for justice. The opposition should be treated to a show. Thus: they televised the execution. Before a standing-room-only crowd, in close-up. Let the whole nation watch. Let them watch, and let them think.

Let them watch.

Let them think.

HIGH TIME CONTINUED, OR THE PLAN OF THE NEXT UNWRITTEN BOOK, ETC.

9

I was thinking of weaving into this book a dictionary of various phrases that take on different meanings according to the degree of geographical latitude, and which serve to define things that have similar names but distinct appearances. Such a dictionary would look more or less like this:

10

SILENCE. People who write history devote too much attention to so-called events heard round the world, while neglecting the periods of silence. This neglect reveals the absence of that infallible intuition that every mother has when her child falls suddenly silent in its room. A mother knows that this silence signifies something bad. That the silence is hiding something. She runs to intervene because she can feel evil hanging in the air. Silence fulfills the same role in history and in politics. Silence is a signal of unhappiness and, often, of crime. It is the same sort of political instrument as the clatter of weapons or a speech at a rally. Silence is necessary to tyrants and occupiers, who take pains to have their actions accompanied by quiet. Look at how colonialism has always fostered silence; at how discreetly the Holy Inquisition functioned; at the way Leonidas Trujillo avoided publicity.

What silence emanates from countries with overflowing prisons! In Somoza's Nicaragua—silence; in Duvalier's Haiti—silence. Each dictator makes a calculated effort to maintain the ideal state of silence, even though somebody is continually trying to violate it! How many victims of silence there are, and at what cost! Silence has its laws and its demands. Silence demands that concentration camps be built in uninhabited areas. Silence demands an enormous police apparatus with an army of informers. Silence demands that its enemies disappear suddenly and without a trace. Silence prefers that no voice—of complaint or protest or indignation—disturb its calm. And where such a voice is heard, silence strikes with all its might to restore the *status quo ante*—the state of silence.

Silence has the capacity of spreading, which is why we use expressions like 'silence reigned everywhere,' or 'a universal silence fell.' Silence has the capacity to take on weight, so that we can speak of 'an oppressive silence' in the same way we would speak of a heavy solid or liquid.

The word 'silence' most often joins words like 'funeral' ('funereal silence'), 'battle' ('the silence after battle') and 'dungeon' ('as silent as a dungeon'). These are not accidental associations.

Today one hears about noise pollution, but silence pollution is worse. Noise pollution affects the nerves; silence pollution is a matter of human lives. No one defends the maker of a loud noise, whereas those who establish silence in their own states are protected by an apparatus of repression. That is why the battle against silence is so difficult.

It would be interesting to research the media systems of the world to see how many service information and how many service silence and quiet. Is there more of what is said or of what is not said? One could calculate the number of people working in the publicity industry. What if you could calculate the number of people working in the silence industry? Which number would be greater?

BLACK. In the Congo, in Stanleyville, there is an old barracks in a side-street that looks something like a small-town fire station. Every Sunday a Kimbangist service is held there. When you walk into the dark interior you feel you have entered the Pechorska Lavra in Kiev because the holy faces in the old icons in old orthodox churches are dark or even, some say, Negro. In the Kimbangist churches the divine faces in the paintings are also black, Negro. The Kimbangists believe that Jesus came into the world as a Negro. So their prophet, Simon Kimbangu, taught them. Kimbangu was born among the Bakong tribe at the end of the last century. On 18 March 1921, he had a vision. He began wandering around the Congo and teaching. He said that he had been sent by God to raise the dead, multiply the loaves and fishes and save the world—that world of jungle and savannah. But God was not white. He was black. The whites had stolen God and for that they would suffer eternal damnation and everlasting torment. This teaching was revolutionary. Kimbangu said: 'Don't listen to Caesar: heed the Word of the Lord!' Kimbangu spoke the language of the Bible because that was all he knew, and his whole programme was served up in an exalted messianic phraseology. At the end of 1921 the Belgians arrested the prophet and sentenced him to death, a sentence which was then commuted to life imprisonment. The persecution of the Kimbangists began. But the stronger the repression, the stronger the movement became. Simon the Prophet had a little church in the jungle. At its opening, he had brought in a bowl of paint. The paint was black. Divine images had hung in the church, and Simon the Prophet went from picture to picture staining the immobile faces of the saints. He changed the bright colours of their foreheads and rosy cheeks, thickened the lips and kinked the hair. When he was finished, the saints had become black, in the image of

Simon and his faithful. That was the first revolutionary gesture in the Congo: smearing pictures with a paintbrush.

SPIRITS. In Africa, many people are still sceptical about the effectiveness of firearms. Every report that someone has been shot to death is received with incredulity. In the first place, no one has ever seen a bullet in flight, so how can it be proved that somebody died because somebody else fired a rifle? Second, there are always methods for reversing the trajectory of a bullet. Various kinds of ju-ju, for instance, are more impervious than steel armour. The former premier of western Nigeria, Chief Akintola, was executed not against a wall, in the usual manner of a firing squad, but in the middle of a large veranda, because his executioners knew that Akintola's ju-ju would have made him impregnable against bullets if he ever managed to touch a wall. Europeans were shocked by reports from the Congo about the desecration of corpses. These were not, as some alleged, acts of sadism. That act of destroying the corpse results from the conviction that a human being consists of not only a body but also the spirits that fill it. Many white people believe in a body and a soul, but their faith in one soul is merely a primitive simplification of a complicated feature of human existence: in reality a person's body is filled by many spirits proper to the various parts of the human organism. It would be naive to believe that this complicated world of spirits, alive in the recesses of the human body, can be liquidated by a single bullet. The body is only one element in a person's death: full death occurs only after the spirits have been destroyed or expelled, and they are expelled in the same way that air is expelled from a balloon: by pricking it. Hence the necessity of destroying the corpse, particularly if the corpse belonged to an enemy whose spirits can later avenge him. There is no cruelty in this—for someone who is forced to fight against the dangerous and omnipresent world of spirits, which may be invisible but are hot on the heels of the living, it is simply self-defence.

HIERARCHY. In Accra, in the buildings of the ministries, the hierarchy of position corresponds to the hierarchy of floors. The higher the personage, the higher the floor. This is because there is a breeze higher up, while down below the air is static, petrified. The petty officials are stifling on the ground floor; the department directors are starting to feel a draught: and at the very top the minister is cooled by that wished-for breeze.

LOCKED UP. Why do guerrillas kidnap diplomats?

The answer is in the context of the Latin American political prisoner's situation. Namely: Whoever protests or fights against the regime is locked up in prison.

The prisoner is not accused of anything. Since he has not been accused, there can be no trial. Since there can be no trial, there is also no verdict. And thus there is no proper sentence. There is no prosecutor, no defence counsel, no appeal, no amnesty. There is no testimony, no indictment, nothing. A witness can be found guilty; the guilty can become innocent, except that this is impossible as there is no court to find anyone not guilty. The situation of the prisoner can be reduced to a simple formula: why is he in prison? Because he has been locked up.

He might be released in a year or in ten years, or he might never be released. Many of these prisoners are let out when the president who locks them up leaves office. Every president has his own prisoners, and their fate is tied to his. A new figure moves into the president's office, and new prisoners fill the cells. That is why certain groups of people—his personal enemies—regularly emigrate with each accession to office of a new president. Otherwise they know they will end up behind bars. Such liberal conditions obtain only in those Latin American countries that have some form of democracy; in the countries ruled by dictators the prisoner has no hope of regaining his freedom or of staying alive.

Take the case of Guatemala. Someone is locked up and tortured. If he survives the torture, he is thrown into prison. There is another series of tortures and an epilogue: a corpse is found in a ditch.

There is no way to defend or rescue a prisoner legally. The law does not extend to him. Liberating a prisoner by force is in fact impossible: the political prisons of Guatemala are located on barracks grounds, and one prisoner is guarded by dozens of armed soldiers, tanks, cannons.

Only one method remains: to kidnap an enemy and exchange him for the prisoner. The action is not carried out haphazardly; they do not kidnap the first person they come across. The target is established after long deliberation, after discussion.

FORTRESS. This is an imposing building, erected in Accra at a cost of over twenty million dollars (at a time when it was hard to buy bread in the city) for the sole purpose of hosting a four-day meeting of African leaders in 1966. After the conference the structure was locked up and now stands empty, falling into disrepair. In the tropics, an unused building turns into a ruin in a few years.

The idea of putting up this edifice, called State House, was Nkrumah's. The architects drew up plans—aimed at creating a building that would combine the height of monumentality with blinding modernity and maximum security. They realized their intentions. State House is gigantic. It stands twelve storeys high. Its annexes contain an enormous meeting hall and an enormous reception hall, and the main building is divided into sixty suites. Each chief of state and each foreign minister has one suite, and each suite consists of ten rooms, with two bathrooms, foyer, etc. The suites are furnished in the most refined splendour.

Even more striking is the security system. Once inside, you find yourself protected by a wall wherever you go, wherever you stand. It is laid out on the model of the toy called the 'Russian grandmother'. In the biggest grandmother there nests a smaller one, and inside the smaller one an even smaller one, and so on. This is the same. Behind the first wall there is a second wall, and behind the second wall a third wall, and in the middle is the suite. In this way, the leaders are protected against attack. Hand weapons would do nothing. A bullet would ricochet off the walls, as would light and medium artillery and mortars up to 160mm. Nothing less than naval artillery or mass aerial bombing could make a dent in the fortress of State House. But such an eventuality was also provided for. Below State House are massive underground shelters with passageways connecting to the rest of the building. The shelters have electricity, lighting, running water, ventilation, etc. Here the leaders are safe even from bombs.

Unless somebody dropped an A-bomb.

In recognition of the fact that sieges can drag on, sufficient food supplies are furnished so that the leaders could not be starved out. In the right wing of State House there is an enormous refrigerated chamber in which enough food to last several months can be stored. Supplies of medicine, water and drinks are also stockpiled. State House has two independent energy sources (a power station and its own generators), as well as independent telephone cables connecting it to important world capitals.

One hardly need add that State House has its own pool, its own cafés, bars and restaurants, its own printing press, central air conditioning, a post office and television. A system has also been devised to protect it against an attack from within, in case of some fifth column uprising, and, in anticipation of this the corridors are neither straight nor interconnected, but winding, broken up, ellipsoidal, descending, zigzag, semi-circular, curved. In this way no attacker could ever take in a whole floor in his sights because a victim would need only to jump around the corner to be safe.

For security reasons it is forbidden to photograph State House, either close-up or from a distance and, if you did, the police would lock you up. Nor is it permitted to stop in front of State House and look at it for long: your papers would be checked and you would be chased away.

STATE VISIT. In 1862, during his expedition in search of the source of the Nile, Speke reached Uganda, where he visited the Baganda king, Mutesa. Alan Moorehead writes:

> Speke set up his chair in front of the throne, erected his umbrella and awaited events. Nothing happened. For an hour the two men sat gazing at one another . . .
> At length a man approached with a message: had he seen the King?
> 'Yes,' Speke answered, 'for full one hour.'
> When this was translated to Mutesa he rose and walked away into the interior of his palace.'

LIFE. The dictatorship of General Abbuda in the Sudan lasted six years. His regime fell on 21 October 1964. It was a harsh but superficial regime, with no mass support. Someone I met in Khartoum told me what happened after 21 October:

It was an extraordinary spectacle. Within three days Khartoum looked exactly the way it had looked the week before Abbuda took power, the way it had looked in 1958. All the old political parties reappeared immediately. Exactly the same parties, under the same names, with the same people. The same newspapers as before began to appear, with the same titles, the same typefaces and editorial stances. The janitors returned and started cleaning the parliament buildings on their own. The politicians immediately resumed the quarrels that had been broken off six years earlier in mid-sentence. Everything looked as if those six years of Abbuda's government had never occurred. Those six years were only an interruption of something that is still continuing, whose thread has been picked up again and is being woven anew.

10

Yet I have not written a dictionary or a book because whenever I start, taking a deep breath and crossing myself as if getting ready to jump into deep water, a red light starts blinking on the map—the signal that at some point on this overcrowded, restless, and quarrelsome globe, something is again happening, the earth quivering, staggering, because this relentless current, this stream of events—it is so difficult to step out of it on to a calm shore—keeps rushing and hurtling by, pulling me under.

11

The editor-in-chief of *Kultura*, Dominik Horodynski, telephones to say that there is money and I can go to the Middle East (the Arab-Israeli war is on; it is late 1973). A few months later the Turks occupy half of Cyprus, on which island a worthy person will smuggle me in his car from the Greek to the Turkish side. I am returning from Cyprus when Janusz Roszkowski, the head of the Polish Press Agency, tells me that it is the last moment to try to get to Angola. I have to hurry before Luanda becomes a closed city. It will be five minutes to twelve when the Portuguese air force lifts me out of Lisbon on board a military transport.

12

Pack the suitcase. Unpack it, pack it, unpack it, pack it: typewriter (Hermes Baby), passport (SA 323273), ticket, airport, stairs, airplane, fasten seat-belt, take off, unfasten seat-belt, flight, rocking, sun, stars, space, hips of strolling stewardesses, sleep, clouds, falling engine speed, fasten seat-belt, descent, circling, landing, earth, unfasten seat-belts, stairs, airport, immunization book, visa, customs, taxi, streets, houses, people, hotel, key, room, stuffiness, thirst, otherness, foreignness, loneliness, waiting, fatigue, life.

BOOTS

I met him in Damascus, in the elevator of a small hotel. He is a Palestinian, but he looks as if he has come straight from Siberia. Felt boots, a heavy coat tied with a belt, a fur cap with ear-flaps. Fortunately, the evenings are chilly in Damascus and you can walk around in a thick quilted jacket without roasting inside it. During the elevator ride, he reaches into his bag and hands me an apple. The Palestinian way of making acquaintances: offer fruit to the person you've just met. Fruit is the largest, and in fact the only, natural wealth of Palestine, and to give someone fruit is to give him everything you have.

He invites me to his room. He is the commander of one of the *fedayeen* groups that are fighting on Mount Hermon. It would be out of place to ask for his name or any details connected with his identity. He is from Galilee, let that suffice.

They have to dress warmly on the front, in down coats and ear-flaps, because Hermon is a mountain the same height as Mount Olympus, covered in snow and raked by icy winds. People die of exposure at night. And sometimes, when the shelling is heavy during the day, they lie motionless for hours and freeze to the rock. Unfortunately, they cannot get used to the snow or the cold; they might as well be fighting on an alien planet. The mountain keeps changing hands. Whoever takes the summit plants his flag there. Then another battle takes place, and, usually, a change of flags. Whoever dies, stays on the mountain, but it is worst for the wounded: there is no way to carry them down and they suffer a lot, because cold magnifies pain.

The *fedayeen* are waging their Palestinian war in the snows of Mount Hermon. The fiercest fighting takes place on the mountain, at short range, face to face, with both sides on the same piece of rock, on a narrow ledge from which one pushes the other over the precipice.

At the foot of the precipice stretches softly folded country, grey, naked, ruined country: this is the Golan Heights. There, the war between Israel and Syria goes on.

The commander from Mount Hermon asks me what I think about the battles on the Golan Heights, what I think about this war.

I tell him that I have never seen such a war.

Our war looked different and it ended long ago, in Berlin, in front of the Brandenburg Gate in 1945. It was a war of millions and millions of people. The trenches stretched for an unending number of kilometres. Even today, you can find traces of fortifications in every Polish forest. Each person made an enormous effort to survive that war; we dug up our whole country with our own hands. When the order to attack came, the soldiers broke out of the trenches like ants, and a great human mass covered the fields, filling the forests and the roads. You could meet people carrying guns everywhere. In my country, the war did not pass anyone by; it went through every home, it smashed its rifle butt against every door, it burned dozens of cities and thousands of villages. The war wounded everyone, and those who survived cannot cure themselves of it. A person who lived through a great war is different from someone who never lived through any war. They are two different species of human beings. They will never find a common language, because you cannot really describe the war, you cannot share it, you cannot tell someone: Here, take a little bit of my war. Everyone has to live out his own war to the end. War is the most brutal of things for a simple reason: it demands horrendous sacrifices. The people from my country that made it to the Brandenburg Gate can say how much victory costs.

Anybody who wants to know how much you have to pay to win a war should look at our cemeteries. Anyone who says that you can achieve a lasting victory without great losses, that you can have the war without the cemeteries, does not know what he is talking about. I want to emphasize the following: the essence of war lies in the fact that war gathers everyone under its black wings. Nobody can remain on the sidelines, nobody can sit drinking coffee when the moment comes to be throwing grenades. Every Algerian took part in the Algerian war. Every Vietnamese took part in the Vietnam war. The Arabs have never waged such a war against Israel.

Why did the Arabs lose the 1967 war? A lot has been said on that subject. You could hear that Israel won because Jews are brave and Arabs are cowards. Jews are intelligent, and Arabs are primitive. The Jews have better weapons, and the Arabs worse. All of it untrue! The Arabs are also intelligent and brave and they have good weapons. The difference lay elsewhere—in the approach to war, in varying theories of war. In Israel, everybody takes part in war, but in the Arab countries—only the army. When war breaks out, everyone in Israel goes to the front and civilian life dies out. While in Syria, many people did not find out about the 1967 war until it was over. And yet Syria lost its most important strategic area, the Golan Heights, in that war. Syria was losing the Golan Heights and at the same time, that same day, that same hour, in Damascus—twenty kilometres from the Golan Heights—the cafés were full of people, and others were walking around, worrying about whether they would find a free table. Syria lost fewer than 100 soldiers in the 1967 war. A year earlier, 200 people had died in Damascus during a palace *coup*. Twice as many people die because of a political quarrel as because of a war in which the country loses its most important territory and the enemy approaches within shooting distance of the capital.

The front line soldier might be better or worse, but every soldier is: a person. A young man runs a particular risk, because his full life is just beginning. And now the whole world crashes down on this person. Death attacks him from all sides. Mines go off under his feet, bullets whistle through the air, bombs drop from the sky. It is very difficult to endure in such a hell. We know that, aside from the worst enemy, there exists an even worse enemy: loneliness in the face of death. The soldier cannot be alone; he will never hold out if he feels like a man under a sentence, if he knows that his brother is sitting in a nightclub playing dominoes, his other brother is horsing around in a swimming pool, and somebody else is worrying about how to find a free table. He must have the feeling that what he is doing is necessary to someone, that it is important to someone, that someone is watching him and someone is helping him, is with him. Otherwise, the soldier will throw everything down and go home.

War cannot be a matter for the army alone, because the burden of war is too great and the army itself will not manage to support it. The Arabs thought otherwise and—they lost. I told the commander from Mount Hermon that I was struck in the Arab world by the drastic gap, by the complete lack of contact between the front and the country, between the life of a soldier and the life of a shopkeeper during the war—they existed in two different worlds and they had different problems—one of them was thinking about how to live through another hour, and the other was thinking about how to sell his merchandise, and these are very different worries indeed.

We went out into the city. Our hotel stood near the main post office and the train station in the busy centre of

Damascus. A long line of shoeshine boys sat in front of the post office building. This place is green with soldiers' uniforms. The fighting on the Golan Heights lasts from daybreak until dusk, and in the evening the soldiers drive into Damascus. They walk the streets in groups, buy something in a shop and usually go to a movie. But before, they stop in front of the post office to have their boots shined. The Golan Heights are dust, which is why the soldiers' boots are always grey, always in need of the brush. The boys that bestow elegance on the soldiers' boots know everything about the war. Terribly dusty boots—there was heavy fighting. Dusty boots, but, ach, only so-so—quiet on the front. Wet boots, as if they'd been pulled out of the water—the *fedayeen* are fighting on Mount Hermon, where there is snow. Boots stinking of diesel oil, smeared with grease—there must have been an armoured clash, and the tank crews have had a rough day.

Boots—these are the war communiqués.

The commander from Mount Hermon remarks that you can see so many soldiers at once only in Damascus, and on the other side probably in Haifa or Tel Aviv, because the army is not visible on the Golan Heights. Both armies are dug into the ground, in bunkers or shelters, or buttoned up inside the armour of their tanks. Nobody walks along the Heights, nobody runs there, you cannot meet a soul on the roads, and the villages are destroyed—an emptiness like the surface of the moon. Whoever wants to see soldiers fighting like in the old days has to scramble up Mount Hermon.

Times have changed now, and the face of war has changed. Man has been removed from the field of vision on the battlefield. We see equipment. We see tanks, self-propelled artillery, rockets and aircraft. Officers push buttons in a bunker, observe the jumps of a green line across a screen, manipulate a joy-stick and press another button: a boom, whistling, and somewhere in the distance a tank disintegrates, somewhere in the sky an airplane flies to pieces.

The ordinary human face has disappeared from the image of war. 'Hey, Dick!' the chief of the Camera Press office shouts over the telephone to his photographer, who is working on the Golan Heights, 'quit sending me rockets all the time. Send me a picture of the living mug of one of those guys that are slugging it out up there!'

But the living mugs are hidden behind the view-slits of the tanks.

THERE WILL BE NO PARADISE

Straight off the plane, they push me into a car and set off, racing along a winding road, not telling me where we are going. The Greek next to me finally says that we are on our way to a refugee camp, a rally, and we might be late. He checks his watch and scolds the driver. This is my first trip to Cyprus, and the beauty of the island has already gone to my head. We are speeding over hill after hill; cypress trees line the road; there are endless vineyards; the villages are of white limestone; the sea beyond them—always the sea.

A quarter of an hour and we turn into a space, flat, big, covered with tents, and a large crowd is standing at one end of it. Someone is on the platform waving his hands, the loudspeakers reverberating with a speech that I cannot understand. The people with me (I don't know their names) start pushing through the crowd, pulling me along; in the crush I smell that stuffy, peasant smell, milk, wool, something else; and then I see their faces, silent, intense, rocky, sallow. The Greek who is pulling me through the crowd by my hand says these are all refugees from the north, poor people without—he adds, clearing the way now with his elbow—houses or possessions. But these are hardly the conditions for a longer conversation, if only because, before I can grasp what is going on, I have been pushed on to the platform and handed a microphone by a young man.

Speak, says someone else. I'll translate.

I am sure that there has been a mistake, that they have taken me for someone else—a dignitary, a minister, an international figure who is meant to tell these unfortunate people about their fate and about who will improve their lot.

The sun is intense and I am soaked with sweat.

I want to get down off the platform and clear up the misunderstanding with the organizers. I am not going to speak; public speaking is torture for me. I know nothing about Cyprus; I have only been here half an hour. I do not know these people and I have nothing to say—at least nothing they couldn't live without.

There is no organizer in sight. There is nobody to whom I can explain the misunderstanding. There are children clinging all around the edge of the platform, like bees on a honeycomb, making it impossible to get down. The crowd is waiting, silently. I stand in this silence; thousands of people are watching me, stupid, lost, trapped. I wipe my face with my handkerchief, playing for time, trying to collect my thoughts. The one who handed me the microphone and the other one who offered to translate are both starting to look impatient. The chidren are staring at me with particular attention.

I have the presence of mind to look around me. The men stand close to the rostrum. Powerful, massively built peasants with angular heads and black, closely-cropped hair. They are unemployed. The war has cut them off from work and deprived them of their fields, their orchards. What could this man have been yesterday? A sower in the spring, a harvester in the fall, the lord of himself all year round. And today? A refugee, with a bowl in his hand, queueing for soup. What a waste of human energy, I think, an abasement of dignity. The peasants on the outskirts of Lima and Bogota, or the ones in India and Thailand, or the young people in Nigeria and Kenya: a billion people capable of work with nothing or almost nothing to do for the duration of their lives. Nobody needs them or wants them in a world where there is already so much to be done. If they could be given worthwhile occupations, humanity could make dizzying progress. The world's wealth would be doubled. Pyramids of merchandise would rise in even the poorest countries. Granaries would overflow. Water would flood the largest deserts. And here, on Cyprus (I want to tell them), couldn't we perform miracles and make your island—a paradise of nature—into a paradise of affluence and plenty? But the war has destroyed everything you had. It has cut down the trees in your orchards and trampled your fields, torn off the roofs of your houses and scattered your sheep. And now the war has sentenced you to be idle spectators of your own misfortune.

Behind the dense mass of peasant men stand the crowd of women, dressed in black, with black scarves on their heads. They are all old.

At the edge of the field there are tents upon tents—the refugee camp. I have seen camps of this kind. The most terrible were outside Calcutta, filled by Hindi shadows that had fled East Pakistan. I say 'shadows' because that throng of skeletons, even while still moving, no longer belonged to the human world. There are Palestinian camps in Jordan, there are the camps of starved nomads in Africa, who having lost their pastures and their cattle—the basis of their existence—are now listless, desolate, waiting for death. Around the cities of Latin America the camps are human hills of poverty. These people have fled the hunger and animal drudgery of the villages, hoping that somewhere, anywhere, even in a refugee camp, it will be better, that they will salvage their lives and find their place.

Dear friends, I say, I have seen much misfortune in my life and here I see more. Our world does not smile on everyone and when it is good in one place, it is bad in another. The trouble is that we do not know how to get off the see-saw. There is no sense in going on about it. There are always dark clouds and we can never know where and when these clouds will produce a deluge. You are this time victims of the deluge. The deluge on Cyprus has taken the form of an armed invasion; a foreign army has seized your villages. I understand your despair, because I come from a country that has known many invasions. The roads of my country have been trod upon by millions of refugees, and in every great war my country has lost everything. I myself have been a refugee, and I know what it means to have nothing, to wander into the unknown and wait for history to utter a kind word. I know that what you care about most right now can be reduced to the questions: when will we recover our homes? when will we return to our land? I want to tell you honestly that I do not know. It may be in a month; it may be never. Your fates are entangled in a great political game, and I cannot foresee how that game will turn out. That is why I am standing here, on this platform, uselessly. I did not come here to promise anything. I came here to get to know you and I hope you will tell me what happened. I propose that we end this rally, and perhaps one of you will invite me to your tent.

I express my thanks, but I have made for a commotion, because the programme calls for many more speakers. An activist of some kind calls on the people to stay and announces the remaining events. I go to those old women dressed all in black. One of them leads me to her tent, and several others follow. They sit me in a chair, although they remain standing. I ask the interpreter why they are standing and am told that they will sit down once a man tells them to. They give me coffee and water. They are Greek peasants from the northern province of Cyprus. Hard-working, worn down by housekeeping and bearing children. Tactlessly, I begin asking about their ages. They are forty or fifty years old, but they look like elderly women. People live long here but spend half of their lives being old. Youth, prolonged endlessly in western Europe, seems not to exist here. First there is a little girl in school, and then immediately a dignified mother surrounded by a pack of children with big, beautiful eyes and their thumbs in their mouths, and a moment later there is this kind of old lady, dressed in black.

I ask these women what hurt them most. They say nothing and cover their faces in their black scarves.

Later they tell me about their sorrow. They tell how suddenly the Turkish army came: it was as if foreign troops had sprung up out of the ground. Airplanes dropped bombs and napalm; tanks rolled along the roads; there were soldiers shooting in all directions. Panic broke out in the villages and people hid in the woods or the hills, wherever they could. Because the Turkish army came from the north, the Greeks began fleeing south. They left everything behind and thought only about saving their lives. Along the road they met Turkish Cypriots heading north. The two streams of people passed each other in silence, both driven by fear, uncertain of what would come next. Houses and vineyards burned all around and they became lost. Nobody knew where they should go, where their people were and how they could reach them.

One of these women is named Maria Salatas. The soldiers killed her husband because he would not tell where he had hidden their two daughters. The soldiers violated any girls who fell into their hands. The local policeman—a Turkish Cypriot—had helped her daughters to hide in the fields. The woman calls these Turkish Cypriots jikimas, which means 'ours' in Greek. Later, Maria was held in a Turkish camp for three months. There was no water and nothing to eat. Turkish Cypriots sneaked food to the Greeks from the village. That village is called Kaputi and the daughters are alive; they are sitting here with us.

Maria and the other women in the tent think that everything was good before the invasion. Of course, you could find hatred in the villages, but the Greeks and the Turks were used to it. They accepted it. It was a part of their lives; it was an internal, communal affair. An equilibrium of hatred existed in the villages and people knew when to back off to avoid a catastrophe. The Greeks of the village never set out to finish off the Turks and the Turks would never set out after the Greeks. Sometimes the boys would go after each other, and then somebody would be hurt, sometimes killed. But it is the same all over the world. Anyone who knows peasant life knows how starved for events a village is, even if it has to pay for them with its own blood. Is that any reason for the Turkish army to come in with tanks and send the Greks into exile? They want the army to leave so that things can be as they were. Nobody picks the oranges, the grapes have rotted on the vines, the cattle have surely been butchered and the meat eaten.

They ask me if I know anything about the missing.

I know nothing.

They ask everyone. Several thousand young Greeks disappeared during the invasion. Whether they are alive, where they are—nobody has an answer. There is no proof that they died, but there is no proof that they are alive. The Turks say they know nothing about them. So where are they? Cyprus is a small island; you could hide ten people here, but not several thousand. They cannot bring themselves to think that those boys are buried somewhere. After all, nobody has seen their graves. Someone said that they were taken out to sea and sunk, but the mind cannot accept such things.

They then showed me their tents. They apologized for the poverty. If I had come earlier, they could have showed me their houses. They had everything in their houses: light and running water and furniture. There was always a garden, and they never ran out of fruit. They talked about these houses, about their villages, as if they were talking about a lost paradise. Their lives had been broken and they did not know to whom to turn. They asked the men, but the men said nothing, shrugging their shoulders. Men can go out into the world and live anywhere, but a woman cannot live without a home. Such a thing was unheard of.

Evening, night and dawn in Nicosia. Nicosia: charming and sunny and bright. A splendid architecture; just looking at the buildings is a pleasure. Goods from all over the world fill the shops; the Cypriot industry is small, and everything has to be imported. Here and there, traces of the invasion: a wall full of bullet holes, an empty window frame, a burnt-out car. But the city's losses are not great. People went to work during the days of the invasion, and shops stayed open.

'During the whole war,' a Polish woman tells me, thinking of the invasion of July and August 1974, 'I saw people lined up only once. For a porno film.'

All day, beginning in the morning, the Greeks sit in chairs in front of the little cafés. Until noon they sit facing the sun; at noon they pull the chairs into the shade; in the afternoon they move back into the sun. These are the men—no women. They sit in silence, without a word, not moving, often with their backs turned to each other, but some sort of unseen community exists among them, because when a Greek comes up to one of them from the street and starts to argue, they all begin to argue.

At dusk the beautiful girls come out for their walk. The girls cannot walk alone; their mothers or grandmothers accompany them. They cannot look around, because that is in bad taste; it creates the impression that they are hunting for boys. The eyes of their mothers or grandmothers are proud, but also wary. From the café terraces, the girls are watched by United Nations soldiers: Swedes, Danes, Finns, big blond boys pink from the sun—good matches, but who can tell if their intentions are honourable? None of these blond boys gets up from the tables, though. They sit drinking their beer, bored, sloppy. Their fair, dull eyes follow the girls until they disappear around a bend in the street.

In the evening the city empties out and falls dead. It gets chilly. Nobody on the streets, empty pavements, locked gates. Darkness and silence on the border between the Greek and Turkish sectors. One spotlight illuminates the rolls of barbed wire. A second illuminates the Turkish flag. A third—the Greek flag. Beneath the Turkish flag, a soldier. Beneath the Greek flag, a soldier. Silent, hunched up against the cold, machine-guns in their numb hands.

In the morning, we are on the Turkish side. In Nicosia there is one crossing between the Greek and Turkish parts of the city, where the street is piled with sandbags and the nearby houses are empty, their windows broken. The Turkish district is poor, with many clay huts and less traffic. The Turkish argument is that the Greeks were unfair, that they were marginalized by them.

A Greek is a skilful merchant; he is a quick, agile intelligence.

A Turk: he needs time to think; he is closed, slow, patient like an Asian.

The Greek will outsmart the Turk in commerce.

The Turk will defeat the Greek on the front.

From Nicosia we drive north into the land occupied by the Turkish army. A countryside of fairy-tale beauty, with a road that first climbs into the hills, then falls between hanging rocks into a forest and then, suddenly, around a turn, the sapphire sea. Below stands miracles of Mediterranean architecture: the old port of Cyrenia, the white houses, the red roofs, the orange groves. There are no half tones; all the colours are violent, colliding, glaring and shocking.

The little streets of Cyrenia are empty and many of the houses destroyed with their doors hanging, blown in. A *gendarme* stands straight as a pillar on every street corner. White helmet, white gloves, blue leggings. He is directing traffic that does not exist. On the Port, it is quiet; the hotels are closed; splendid yachts are taking water. In a shop, you can buy a postcard that shows Cyprus as a part of Turkey.

Everywhere on the road are troops and more troops. This is an enormous army on manoeuvres. Tanks in motion, self-propelled guns in firing position, fighters at tree-top level. Platoons on the march, companies at double time, battalions attacking. Here is a brigade digging in on open ground, and there is a division storming a rock face.

This is a threatening army, in a state of constant readiness. There is nothing like it on the Greek side; it is hard to find a Greek soldier.

Nicosia, night, ten minutes after midnight.
A shot rings out on the Greek side.
The silence lasts for a second.
Then come three shots from the Turkish side.
Next, from the Greeks: ten.
And a hundred from the Turks.
And five hundred from the Greeks.
And a thousand from the Turks.
And a cannon from the Greeks.
And a heavier cannon from the Turks.

So 125's from the Greeks.
But 164's from the Turks.
Thus incendiaries from the Greeks.
To which, from the Turks, fragmentation.

One side opens fire with everything it has, and so does the other at the same time, as if on command, suddenly, who knows why, for no reason, senselessly, without logic a sleepy sentry might have dozed with his finger on the trigger or it might have been some lunatic, some provocateur, or somebody just felt like it, on a whim, and that was enough, that one shot at ten minutes past midnight, to plunge the whole of Nicosia into a hell made of cross-fire in the course of one minute, into an exploding elemental fury that falls on the drowsy city like a fiery apocalyptic rain.

I jump out of bed in my room on the sixth floor of the Nicosia Palace Hotel and look out the window. Two waves of tracers are breaking against each other over the roofs of the city. The walls tremble and the windows sing. People are running up the stairs, dashing through the streets, ducking into doorways. Nobody knows what is going on or what it is about.

It isn't about anything.

It is a matter of that one shot.

Everybody is on his feet at UN headquarters. The alarm is sounding in the UN barracks. UN liaison officers get the Greeks and Turks to agree on a ceasefire as of 0:45. At 0:45 the fire-fight goes quiet. But the order has not reached all the outposts; some Turk is still firing, and so the Greeks resume fire, and then the Turks open up with everything they have, and there is such a noise that you can't hear anything, and that hellish cacophony goes on into its second hour with people taking cover in cellars, lying on the floors, in shelters, under cars, and those who live closest to the front are scrambling towards the far ends of the city, while the UN gets the Greeks and the Turks to agree to a ceasefire as of 2:05, and again the fire-fight pauses, but this time some Greek has not received the order and keeps banging away with his machine-gun so that for a moment only his lonely series is trickling across the sky, but that's enough for the Turks to go on, and so one more time they open up, tirelessly, letting the Greeks have it, and now the Greeks come back with the full force of their fire, with all the steel they can throw, and for the third time the UN arranges a ceasefire, for 2:45, and this time the order gets all the way down the line, the shooting stops, and silence envelops the city.

The morning after that night, the Greeks are sitting motionless outside the little cafés, saying nothing, as if nothing had happened. At noon, they move into the shade. At dusk, the beautiful girls come out for their walk, accompanied by their mothers and grandmothers. The big blonds from the UN watch them, but they do not move and keep drinking their beer. In the evening the city empties and there is nobody on the streets. Two soldiers, a Greek and a Turk, stand at the border between the sectors. They stand in silence, hunched up against the cold, with machine-guns in their numb hands.

THE OGADEN: AUTUMN '76

A scorpion bit me at night. I crawled into the tent in the close, stifling darkness and lay down on the cot. Neither flashlight nor matches. Anyway, the commandant is ordering us to cut down on light so that we don't give away the position of our camp. They might be lying in a ring a step away and waiting, with their eyes to their gun-sights.

Something moved suddenly on the sheet in the place where I had put my head. I thought it was a lizard. It could not be a cobra, because the movement was too light, too feeble. One more twitching of something close to me, a rustling, and silence again, dead. It went on like that, quiet, soundless, invisible, but I could feel that it was going on very near, even coming nearer. Suddenly there was an explosion in my forehead, deafening, as if someone had smashed my head with a hammer. Excruciating. I leapt up and started to scream: Scorpion! Scorpion!

Marcos ran in a moment later, and then the soldiers. One of them turned on a flashlight. A flat, grey, venomous repulsiveness lay on the sheet. The soldiers cautiously gathered up the sheet, put it on the ground, and began to stamp on the scorpion. Others looked on, as if they were observing a ritual dance for the expulsion of an evil spirit.

My face began to puff up instantly. The soldier shone his flashlight at me and now they all looked gravely at my violently swelling head which was growing like dough in a mixing bowl, the eyes getting smaller and smaller until they must have vanished, sunk, because I stopped seeing. They looked at me standing before them: a hundred mouths, monstrous, wailing in pain, not belonging to myself, isolated from me.

But what could be done? Scorpions sting people like mosquitoes. Those who took a heavy dose of venom died.

From here to the nearest hospital was two days on the road. Lie down, said Marcos. They left me alone in the tent. I sat on the cot afraid to move, so that I would not agitate the scorpions, not give them any sign of myself. They crawled along the ground in the darkness, up the flaps of the tent, dragging their barbed abdomens behind. From that night on, through my whole stay in Ogaden, I could not free myself of them. They spawned in the sands, emerged from under rocks, lurked on the trails. I wanted to get out of there, but we were imprisoned in the desert and had to wait for a chance to escape.

Marcos and I flew to Gode in a light airplane. Disembarking from the airplane was like riding a coal-shovel towards a stove. We escaped straight under the wings, into the shade. The police came and began the body search, the poking, the pawing, looking for guns, checking passes. I did not have a pass. My predicament was ambiguous. I had flown from Addis Ababa at the last moment, without any certainty that I would reach Ogaden—a province closed to foreigners. Go ahead, said Y from the Ministry of Information, I'll send word by radio to let you in. I met the boy named Marcos in the airplane. He was carrying pesticides to be used against some insect that nibbled corn. I thought that if I stuck close to Marcos, he would pull me through all the checkpoints. To buy my way into his favour, I helped him carry the box full of pesticide. In general, I behaved as if I had been assigned to him officially. I tagged along somewhat impudently, but I had no Ethiopian documents and I knew no one in Ogaden. How was I going to get around without a car in that hell where walking a hundred metres is a major effort, and where was I going to sleep, since there are no hotels there?

But what I feared most were the suspicions of the police and the soldiers. A white man in this front line zone at the end of the world—what's he doing here?

Show your papers.

I have no papers.

Well, then, let's go to the barracks for the interrogation.

The airplane took off, leaving us alone in the sun with the pesticide. We covered our heads with newspapers so that we could stand the molten heat, so that we wouldn't fall over, it was so hot. The Ogaden desert burned all around and now, high noon, there was no sign of life. We were looking at the most uncomplicated of images, reduced to two planes: at the bottom—a band of earth; higher, into infinity—the expanse of the sky. In the middle, two drops of sweat—Marcos and I.

We waited a long time until a Land-Rover drove up and a tiny bearded man got out. That's Getahun, the commandant, Marcos told me. We loaded the box as if we were in a slow-motion film, every movement an ordeal, and we drove off in an unknown direction, like a boat wandering over the sea. They spoke in Amharic and I understood not a word. We moved slowly through billows of dust, our vehicle pitching from side to side.

'So who are you?' asked Getahun.

I told him.

'Do you have a paper?'

'No, but they're sending word by radio.'

He fell silent, and later he went on talking with Marcos. We were in the drought zone. In the place where the Ethiopian government was organizing camps for the starving and the thirsty, for those who had managed to save themselves from death. A few peop e, like Getahun and Marcos, were fighting their own war here for the lives of the dying nomads.

Every morning Getahun went to the camp to urge the people to go out into the desert. We'll dig a canal, he would say, the water will flow, the corn will grow. They did not know what a canal looks like or how corn grows. A murmur would go around the crowd and Getahun would turn to the interpreter to ask what they wanted.

They do not want corn. Their diet is meat and milk. They want camels.

But don't you see, Getahun would say, your camels died off.

Yes, that is true, it all happened by the will of Allah.

The crowd then melted away, disappearing somewhere into their shelters, into the bushes, collapsing into the shade. Getahun did not give up. So he began from the beginning, every day. There was inexhaustible patience on both sides—his explaining and their listening. Weeks passed and nothing happened. They received a daily ration of a half-kilogram of corn. They ate part of it, because they had nothing else, and they set some of it aside without telling anyone and sold it on the black market: they were saving up for camels. Whoever managed to save up the price of a camel, or even a few goats, would disappear into the desert. Often this meant certain doom, death from thirst, never seeing anyone again, but nature was stronger than the instinct of self-preservation. For them, life meant movement, conquering space, and when they stayed in one place they withered up and died.

At the end of the nineteenth century, Emperor Menelik of Ethiopia extended his control over regions to the east and south of the territory that traditionally made up the land of Ethiopia. One of his conquests in this campaign was the province of Ogaden, which the Ethiopians today call the province of Harer and which the Somalis call Western Somalia. Since the inhabitants of Ogaden are Somali nomads, Somalia demands the return of the province.

The border between Ethiopia and Somalia exists only on the map; in fact it can be crossed at will, as long as one does not come into contact with an outpost of one of the armies, and these outposts, few in number, lie at intervals of dozens of kilometres. Neither of these countries has the means or sufficient military forces to guard its border rigorously. It is possible to drive one or two hundred kilometres into the depths of Ethiopia without being detected. The same is true on the Somali side. Fixed points are scarce in this terrain: a few small, impoverished settlements, clay shelters lacking light and plumbing. Whoever holds a settlement controls the entire surrounding territory.

Ogaden is a great semi-desert, a gigantic frying pan in which the sun-scorched air sizzles all day long and the principal human exertion involves the search for shade and a breeze. To find shade is to hit the winning number in the lottery. To find a breeze is to know the taste of joy. To last out a whole day in the sun there seems like a task beyond the strength of man, and in earlier days the most ingenious forms of torture included stripping a white person naked and leaving him alone with the sun.

The total surface area of Ogaden (Ethiopian and Somali combined) is equal to that of Poland. This territory can boast of one more or less tolerable road—which is, nevertheless, too demanding for passenger cars. That road is suitable only for all-terrain vehicles, desert trucks and tanks. There is also one river: the Wabe Shebele Wenz, full of dangerous and voracious crocodiles. Anyone who controls that road and that river can call himself the lord of Ogaden.

The night watch returns at dawn and the day patrols set out into the desert. The officer says that the border is near and that Somalia could attack at any moment. He doubts that they would mount a frontal attack, with the whole army, because the terrain is too rough to wage a regular war. Most often, they send in loose units of soldiers made out to look like partisans. If there are only a few, he regards the situation as normal. If there are many, he regards it as war. Here, the front is always and everywhere.

I ask if these units could overrun a settlement like Gode or K'ebri Dehar.

No, he says—there are strong army garrisons in the settlements, there are tanks and artillery, and the partisan units have to be small because otherwise they would have trouble transporting water. They can attack tiny villages or vehicles on the road, nothing more.

I ask if he remembers the last war.

He says that he does. I also remember. It was 1964. I was in Somalia then. I was sitting in Hargeisa, with no way of reaching Mogadishu. The only stately building in all Hargeisa was the former residence of the British governors. Hargeisa became a large city in the dry season—it had water, which the nomads with their flocks were always chasing. In the spring, when the pastures started to turn green, the city emptied out and turned into a third-class desert stopping-place. Life concentrated around the only petrol station in town. You could get tea there and listen to the radio. From truck drivers passing through—a rare sight—you could find out what was going on in the rest of the country, as well as in the outside world: in Djibouti and

Aden. I went there every day, hoping to encounter a truck that would take me to Mogadishu. For a week the road was empty and nobody appeared. Finally, suddenly, a column of twenty new Land-Rovers emerged out of a cloud of dust. They were driving from Berbera to Mogadishu. I asked the drivers to take me. We drove for five days across an appalling desert, through a dead no-man's land, in clouds of dust that billowed not only behind the vehicles, but also from underneath them, so that the drivers lost all visibility. They did not drive single file, but in a row, across a fiery plain without roads, without people. You could see only your nearest neighbours on the left side and on the right; everything else had vanished into the clouds of dust.

I did not see water for five days. Our only drink, or indeed nourishment, was tart, bitter camel's milk. We acquired that milk from nomads we met along the route. They appeared suddenly out of nowhere. They were wandering with their flocks of camels, goats and sheep in search of pastures and wells.

The terrain that we were driving across was the border of Somalia and Ethiopia, the heart of the Ogaden. Since instead of marked roads there were only lonely rocks and solitary acacias there for the drivers to take bearings from, I asked them exactly which country we were in. They did not know with certainty. That means that, in their opinion, we were in Somalia, since they believed that their country covered the whole desert. Nevertheless, they drove the whole time in anxiety and tension, fearing that we could improvidently stray into the depths of Ethiopia and end up in enemy hands. From time to time we came across fresh signs of the continuing war: burned and devastated settlements, human and animal skeletons picked clean by vultures and scattered around poisoned wells. Whose settlements were they? Ethiopian or Somali? I could not tell. With the wells poisoned, there was no sign of life. The drivers swore vengeance against the Ethiopians, called the Prophet as their witness, and cursed the Emperor in the vilest of words. I rode with my heart in my mouth, dreading an Ethiopian ambush, because our fate could be dreadful. Again we passed abandoned settlements of thatched mud huts, smashed, testifying to fierce, ludicrous fighting. Once, we slept in such a place. At night the hyenas moved in, smelled carrion and raised their mad sneering laughter.

Nevertheless, when Marcos asked me if this was my first time in the Ogaden, I answered that yes, it was my first time. It would not have been pleasant for him to hear that I had seen that war through the eyes of the Somali drivers. That I had trembled in fear of the Ethiopian army. That I had dreamed of our convoy having a Somali army escort. And now everything had turned around. Now I feared that the Somalis would attack our camp. I had nothing against either nation, but circumstances had forced me to take sides in that conflict—first one side and now the other.

We went to where the Somali tents stood. Getahun called a meeting of the council of elders. Four of them came. I started asking them how old they were. The oldest was thirty-four. The unfavourable, indeed hostile, land did not permit them a long life. They said that the year consists of the rainy season, called *gu*, and the dry season—*jilal*. Rain is the sweetness of life. The earth covers itself with grass and the wells fill with water. That is the time for marriages, when the strength comes out in men and a desire for everything awakens in women. But *gu* ends quickly and *jilal* sets in. The sun burns the grass and dries up the wells. Then they have to roll up their tents and set out seeking pasture and water. The season of dangers and wars follows, since the pasture is scant and cannot accommodate all the herds. If some clan wants to occupy a pasture, it must wage war for it. People die so that the livestock can live. Similar wars are fought over wells, since there is too little water to divide among everyone.

Around every well, the ground is full of human bones.

In search of water and pasture, they cross the endless space of the Ogaden. They are always on the road. Because of this imperative to move, the Somali owns nothing aside from his shirt and his gun. There is the Somali, and there is his flock. His wife owns a tent, a tea-kettle, and a pot. They do not accumulate any inanimate objects, which would only be a burden. After all, the chances of survival depend on who reaches the pasture and the wells first. Therefore, their desires run in a direction contrary to the ideals and ambitions of people in the industrialized world. There, people walk through life gathering a thousand things; the Somali discards everything at the side of the road as he walks.

He walks proud, slender, tall, humming verses of the Koran.

In these wanderings he acknowledges no borders; for him the world is not divided into states, but into places where there is water, and therefore life, and places where there is drought, and therefore death. They say that there has been no *gu* for several years, that an eternal *jilal* has prevailed. Everything has changed. For a time they wandered as before, but they found water more and more rarely. The desert grew larger, became enormous, had no boundaries. First the sheep fell, and later the goats. Then the children began to die, and later the asses fell. Next, the women died. Anyone who comes across a tea-kettle or a pot while walking will find the remains of the woman nearby. Next, the camels fell. They—these four thirty-year-old elders—kept going. Or rather, at the beginning there were more than a dozen of them, but the others gradually dropped away, dying of thirst and exhaustion. These four, as well, finally ran out of strength.

They lay in the sun unable to take a single step; one of them sat on a stone.

The one who was sitting up noticed the distant Land-Rover in which people drove around the desert searching for dying Somalis. That was how they found themselves in the camp, where they stealthily hoarded corn so that they could buy camels and return to their world.

Marcos brought word yesterday that a tank truck is going to try to get through to Dire Dawa: 900 kilometres, three days on the road. But the next airplane might not come for two months and there is no other chance to get out of here. It is hazardous since the partisans are mining the roads and getting yourself blown up is easy. We could also run into an ambush, in which case they would either kidnap us or kill us. The discussion lasts all night, since departure is at dawn and we have to decide. The tank truck has to get to Dire Dawy to bring back fuel, which is running low in Gode. Fuel for the pumps that draw water out of the river and into the corn fields. If the pumps stop, the corn will wither and hunger will return. If the tank truck is blown up, then the death that the four elders avoided will catch up with them here.

The officer asks if we are afraid to go.

We are afraid, but what can we do? If only there were a truck full of soldiers. But the soldiers sit in their bases and only move when they have to.

On the other hand, it is better to go without an escort. We are innocent people, on our way to get fuel that is needed to save your Somali brothers.

Yes, but if we hit a mine the whole argument becomes pointless.

At dawn, we drive to the nearby settlement to look for the tank truck. The driver is asleep under his vehicle; we wake him. At that hour, it is even cold.

We set out jammed into the cab, jolting over the rocks and stones at a speed of ten kilometres per hour. Day breaks and the sun shines into our faces.

DISPATCHES

The fire stood between us and linked us together. A boy
added wood and the flames rose higher, illuminating our
faces.

'What is the name of your country?'

'Poland.'

Poland was far away, beyond the Sahara, beyond the sea,
to the north and the east. The *Nana* repeated the name
aloud. 'Is that how it is pronounced?' he asked.

'That's the way,' I answered. 'That's correct.'

'They have snow there,' Kwesi said. Kwesi worked in
town. Once, at the cinema, there was a movie with snow.
The children aplauded and cried merrily, '*Anko! Anko!*'
asking to see the snow again. The white puffs fell and fell.
Those are lucky countries, Kwesi said. They do not need to
grow cotton; the cotton falls from the sky. They call it
snow and walk on it and even throw it into the river.

We were stuck here by this fire by chance—three of us,
my friend Kofi from Accra, a driver and I. Night had
already fallen when the tyre blew—the third tyre, rotten
luck. It happened on a side road, in the bush, near the
village of Mpango in Ghana. Too dark to fix it. You have
no idea how dark the night can be. You can stick out your
hand and not see it. They have nights like that. We walked
into the village.

The *Nana* received us. There is a *Nana* in every village,
because *Nana* means boss, head man, a sort of mayor but
with more authority. If you want to get married back home
in your village, the mayor cannot stop you, but the *Nana*
can. He has a Council of Elders, who meet and govern and
ponder disputes. Once upon a time the *Nana* was a god.
But now there is the independent government in Accra. The
government passes laws and the *Nana* has to execute them.

A *Nana* who does not carry them out is acting like a feudal lord and must be got rid of. The government is trying to make all *Nanas* join the party.

The *Nana* from Mpango was skinny and bald, with thin Sudanese lips. My friend Kofi introduced us. He explained where I was from and that they were to treat me as a friend.

'I know him,' my friend Kofi said. 'He's an African.'

That is the highest compliment that can be paid a European. It opens every door for him.

The *Nana* smiled and shook hands. You always greet a *Nana* by pressing his right hand between both of your own palms. This shows respect. He sat us down by the fire, where the elders had just been holding a meeting. The bonfire was in the middle of the village, and to the left and right, along the road, there were other fires. As many fires as huts. Perhaps twenty. We could see the fires and the figures of the women and the men and the silhouettes of the clay huts—they were all visible against a night so dark and deep that it felt heavy like a weight.

The bush had disappeared, even though the bush was everywhere. It began a hundred metres away, immobile, massive, a tightly packed, coarse thicket surrounding the village and us and the fire. The bush screamed and cried and crackled; it was alive; it smelled of wilted green; it was terrifying and tempting; you knew that you could touch it and be wounded and die, but tonight, this night, you couldn't even see it.

Poland.

They did not know of any such country.

The elders looked at me with uncertainty, possibly suspicion. I wanted to break their mistrust somehow. I did not know how and I was tired.

'Where are your colonies?' the *Nana* asked.

My eyes were drooping, but I became alert. People often asked that question. Kofi had asked it first, long ago, and my answer was a revelation to him. From then on he was always ready for the question with a little speech prepared, illustrating its absurdity.

Kofi answered: 'They don't have colonies, *Nana*. Not all white countries have colonies. Not all whites are colonialists. You have to understand that whites often colonize whites.'

The elders shuddered and smacked their lips. They were surprised. Once I would have been surprised that they were surprised. But not any more. I can't bear that language, that language of white, black and yellow. The language of race is disgusting.

Kofi explained: 'For a hundred years they taught us that the white is somebody greater, super, extra. They had their clubs, their swimming pools, their neighbourhoods, their whores, their cars and their burbling language. We knew that England was the only country in the world, that God was English, that only the English travelled around the globe. We knew exactly as much as they wanted us to know. Now it's hard to change.'

Kofi and I stuck up for each other; we no longer spoke about the subject of skin, but here, among new faces, the subject had to come up.

One of the elders asked, 'Are all the women in your country white?'

'All of them.'

'Are they beautiful?'

'They're very beautiful,' I answered.

'Do you know what he told me, *Nana*?' Kofi interjected. 'That during their summer, the women take off their clothes and lie in the sun to get black skin. The ones that become dark are proud of it, and others admire them for being as tanned as blacks.'

Very good Kofi, you got them. The elders' eyes lit up at the thought of those bodies darkening in the sun, because, you know how it is, boys are the same all over the world: they like that sort of thing. The elders rubbed their hands together, smiled; women's bodies in the sun; they snuggled up inside their loose *kente* robes that looked like Roman togas.

'My country has no colonies,' I said after a time, 'and there was a time when my country was a colony. I respect what you've suffered, but, we too, have suffered horrible things: there were streetcars, restaurants, districts *nur für Deutsch*. There were camps, war, executions. You don't know camps, war and executions. That was what we called fascism. It's the worst colonialism.'

They listened, frowning, and closed their eyes. Strange things had been said, which they needed time to take in.

'Tell me, what does a streetcar look like?'

The concrete is important. Perhaps there was not enough room. No, it had nothing to do with room; it was contempt. One person stepping on another. Not only Africa is a cursed land. Every land can be like it—Europe, America, any place. The world depends on people, needs to step on them.

'But *Nana*, we were free afterwards. We built cities and ran lights into the villages. Those who couldn't read were taught how to read.'

The *Nana* stood up and grasped my hand. The rest of the elders did the same. We had become friends, *przyjaciele, amigos*.

I wanted to eat.

I could smell meat in the air. I could smell a smell that was not of the jungle or of palm or of coconuts; it was the smell of a kielbasa, the kind you could get for 11.60 zlotys at that inn in the Mazury. And a large beer.

Instead we ate goat.

Poland . . . snow falling, women in the sun, no colonies. There had been a war; there were homes to build; somebody teaching somebody to read.

I had told them something, I rationalized. It was too late to go into details. I wanted to go to sleep. We were leaving at dawn; a lecture was impossible. Anyway, they had worries of their own.

Suddenly I felt shame, a sense of having missed the mark. It was not my country I had described. Snow and the lack of colonies—that's accurate enough, but it is not what we know or what we carry around within ourselves: nothing of our pride, of our life, nothing of what we breathe.

Snow—that's the truth, *Nana*. Snow is marvellous. And it's terrible. It sets you free with your skis in the mountains and it kills the drunkard lying by the fence. Snow, because in January, January 1945, the January offensive, there were ashes, ashes everywhere: Warsaw, Wroclaw, and Szczecin. And bricks, freezing hands, vodka and people laying bricks—this is where the bed will go and the wardrobe right here—people filing back into the centre of the city, and ice on the window panes, and no water, and those nights, the meetings till dawn, and angry discussions and later the fires of Silesia, and the blast furnaces, and the temperature—160 degrees centigrade—in August in front of the blast furnaces, our tropics, our Africa, black and hot. Oh, what a load of shit—What do you mean?—Oh, what a lovely little war—Shut up about the war! We want to live, to be happy, we want an apartment, a TV, no, first a motor-scooter—what air! No clouds, no turning back, if Herr Adenauer thinks, too many graves. A Pole can drink and a Pole can fight, why can't we work? What if we never learn how? Our ships are on every sea, success in exports, success in boxing, youngsters in gloves, wet gloves pulling a tractor out of the mud, Nowa Huta, build, build, build, Tychy and Wizow, bright apartments, upward mobility, a cowherd yesterday and an engineer today—Do you call that an engineer? and the whole streetcar burst out laughing. Tell me: what does a streetcar look like? It's very simple: four wheels, an electrical pick-up, enough, enough, it's all a code, nothing but signs in the bush, in Mpango, and the key to the code is in my pocket.

We always carry it to foreign countries, all over the world, our pride and our powerlessness. We know its configuration, but there is no way to make it acessible to others. It will never be right. Something, the most important thing, the most significant thing, something remains unsaid.

Relate one year of my country—it does not matter which one: let us say, 1957. And one month of that year—say, July. And just one day—let us say, the sixth.

No.

Yet that day, that month, that year exist in us, somehow, because we were there, walking that street, or digging coal, or cutting the forest, and if we were walking along that street how can we then describe it (it could be Kraków) so that you can see its movement, its climate, its persistence and changeability, its smell and its hum?

They cannot see it. You cannot see it, anything, the night, Mpango, the thick bush, Ghana, the fire dying out, the elders going off to sleep, the *Nana* dozing, and snow falling somewhere, and women like blacks, thoughts, 'They are learning to read, he said something like that,' thoughts, 'They had a war, ach, a war, he said, yes, no colonies, that country, Poland, white and they have no colonies,' thoughts, the bush screams, this strange world.

AFTERWORD

An Interview with Ryszard Kapuściński, 1987

Bill Buford

Bill Buford: Your first book to be published in English was The Emperor, *which appeared in 1978. But you had been writing for nearly thirty years before your two translators, an American and a Pole, took it upon themselves to translate your book and submit it to an American publisher. What do you feel we should know about those years before the writing of* The Emperor?

Ryszard Kapuściński: For years I have been building up a small collection of books, newspapers and photographs about Pinsk. I would like to show it to you. Pinsk, you see, is the town where I was born and where I lived until I was eight, when the entire area, originally part of Poland, came under Russian control.

The collection is material for an autobiography?

I don't know, maybe. No, it's merely part of a landscape, my landscape, the landscape that I came from. It is the landscape of a flat, a very flat, country, a marshland, and there are two things that are important to me about Pinsk.

First that here in this very provincial town, this town of dirt roads, cut off from everything, was in fact an extraordinary cosmopolitan gathering. Many of the founders of the State of Israel came from my town. There were Jews, Poles, Byelorussians, Ukrainians, Armenians, and every kind of religion, from Judaism to Catholicism to Islam, and we all lived together. The people were called Poleshuks, meaning merely 'people born in the district of Polesie', and they were a people without a nation and without, therefore, a national identity. And, second, while Pinsk was very international – or, if you like, very 'nationless' – it was also very poor.

How?

Poor in the most elementary things. During the war we ate very primitive pastry – flour and water. That was our diet. We never had shoes; we covered our feet with bark. I remember while there were lecturers in philosophy, the only philosophy they could teach was bourgeois philosophy, and the university was therefore prohibited from hiring them. A Marxist philosophy hadn't developed yet.

How much were you aware of the machinations of the government at the time? Of how its members had been trained in Moscow during the war, or of the rigged election in 1947?

Well, I was an activist at the time. We were all activists. Kolakowski, other writers, intellectuals – some of them later emigrated in fact. I can't think of anyone who wasn't an activist. I myself had joined one of the communist youth organizations in 1948.

Because communism was seen as an unequivocally good thing?

Yes. Of course. Among young people, a very good thing. We all thought we were doing the right thing, and we were very committed, very enthusiastic. We were full of hope.

And what was it you hoped to achieve? What were you hoping a Communist government would bring? That the land would be re-distributed or—

Everything. Everything good. Yes, yes, we were full of confidence. You must remember how young we were. It is hard to explain this to young people in Poland today, because they are so much more informed than we ever thought possible: they have access to history, to information, to news. We had none of this. We had no tradition and no books; we were poor – really, very, very poor – and inexperienced and uneducated. And the little education that we did have came from Stalinist texts. Don't forget that I entered university in 1950: the height of the Stalinist era, in which everything was pure, uncompromised Stalinism.

An interest in philosophy, a grounding in history – these are not the obvious disciplines for training a war correspondent. Were you tempted by academia?

I had actually been asked to stay on at the university to teach, but for me scholarship was tedious, a burden. By then I had done quite a bit of writing. I had had my first poem published in *Slowo Powszechne*, a Catholic daily, and had had a number of poems published in the leading literary magazine of the time. On finishing university in 1955, I was twenty-three-years-old, and I began working for *Sztandar Mlodych*, a youth journal, at the most militant time in its history. It was the age of investigative reporting.

And the most important piece to emerge in that time was in fact written by you.

That would be 'This Too is the Truth of Nowa Huta'. Somehow, our paper succeeded in getting my article through, and it was extremely polemical. Nowa Huta was the showcase steel factory being built near Cracow. It was meant to be our economic triumph. But I had worked there as a student. I had friends there. I knew what the conditions were like, and they were appalling. The plant was mismanaged and the supervisors were frequently drunk. The moment the article appeared, there was a great uproar, and I had to go into hiding.

Hiding?

Yes, the workers, who were my friends, protected me. Eventually I was apprehended, fired from the paper and punished.

What kind of punishment?

It is complicated. The uproar, in any event, continued, until finally a commission was appointed to investigate my allegations. It confirmed everything I said, and I was awarded the Golden Cross of Merit. I was just twenty-three.

The experience was an exciting one for me. It illustrated that writing was about risk – about risking everything. And that the value of the writing is not in what you publish but in its consequences. If you set out to describe reality, then the influence of the writing is upon reality.

I find this all a little curious. At the age of twenty-three, you wrote an article, extremely political in its implications, dealing specifically with a Polish subject, which had such an impact that it actually changed government policy. You were then to go on to write a series of stories, some of the most elegant you've written, about life in rural Poland, The Polish Bush, *that became an immediate bestseller. But you seem to have spent the rest of your writing career avoiding Poland. Why?*

It's not that I've avoided Poland. It's just that there are others writing about Poland, and they do it very well. My subject is a different one, for I became fascinated by something else.

Shortly after I was reinstated, I approached the editor of the paper. I had won a prize, and I asked if I could go abroad. I wanted to get out of Warsaw. I wanted to see the world. He asked me where I wanted to go, and I said I wanted to see something different, something exotic.

Like?

Like Czechoslovakia.

Czechoslovakia?

Yes, because for me Czechoslovakia was the big world, it was foreign and far away. Instead, the editor sent me to India.

Had the paper ever sent a correspondent abroad?

Never.

No foreign correspondents?

I was the first.

You mustn't forget that for my generation the outside world did not exist. There was no outside world, or, if there was, we knew little about it. A place like India wasn't a country. Africa wasn't a continent. They were fairy-tales. And I wanted, really, nothing more than the opportunity to see what the world was like.

And after India?

After India, there was Pakistan and Afghanistan. My reports were liked, and so I was then sent to the Far East, to Japan and China, where for a time I worked as the resident foreign correspondent for the paper, and eventually to Africa. It was exciting because I was discovering the world. It is for this reason that years later, in 1968, while compiling a number of pieces that would eventually be published as *The Soccer War*, I insisted they be arranged in the historical order in which they were written. It was important to me to illustrate the experiences by which a foreigner enters a new world – especially the world of Africa. He is, for instance, at first frightened, then surprised – and then he discovers the pleasure, the fun, the exhilaration.

I also remember, while compiling *The Soccer War*, that during my time in Latin America I was always missing my Africa.

Why?

I'm not sure. In part, because Africa was my youth, and, perhaps in saying I miss my Africa, I am actually saying that I am missing my youth. It was in Africa that I really came into my own as a correspondent, for I had very different responsibilities from those of a traditional correspondent.

For a start, I was by then working for PAP, the Polish Press Agency. And I chose to work for a press agency for very specific reasons, because in every other respect working for an agency is pure slavery.

'Hardened cynical men', as you describe them in The Emperor, *'who have seen everything and lived through everything, and who are used to fighting a thousand obstacles that most people could never imagine just to do their jobs'.*

No other journalist – working for a newspaper or magazine or television – has to put up with the horrors that a press agency writer has. One day I will write about them, my friends, these anonymous markers of events, these terrible victims of information, working day and night in the worst of all possible conditions. But I took on this job voluntarily, because I knew that working for a press agency I would see more things, meet more people. A mercenary, a revolutionary, a general is not going to waste his time on a journalist from an obscure newspaper in Poland that he has never heard of – even if it were possible for that obscure newspaper to send a correspondent to see him. But he might grant an interview to a journalist who is reporting to the entire country.

And I also knew that, working for the agency, I could travel more than if working for someone else. Poland is a poor country. It cannot afford many foreign correspondents. Reuters, Associated Press or Agence France-Presse have a correspondent in nearly every African country. While working for Poland, I was asked to be the correspondent for the entire continent. I could not only go wherever I wanted, but it was my job to go wherever I wanted. If there was trouble, I was meant to be there to see it. I am often asked how it was possible that I could have seen so much as a journalist. I have personally witnessed twenty-seven revolutions. It seems impossible but that is precisely what my job required. I was responsible for fifty countries. I was bound to come across something at least once a month, in at least one of those countries. I was full of stories.

I get a sense that you must have been quite an operator.

You had to be. You had to be because the job required it and because, working for a poor agency, your greatest resource was never money – it was information, contacts, who you knew, what you knew.

A journalist working for a wealthy agency can hire a car or an aeroplane at a moment's notice, but I never could. So, for instance, when trouble erupted in Zanzibar, I had to get there, but had no transport. However, unlike the journalists from the big agencies, I knew some people involved in the revolution. They were my friends. One of the big agency journalists asked for my help. He had the aeroplane but no permission to land. So I made a deal: 'Okay, Felix, I have no money to hire a plane. But if you take me with you, I'll arrange the clearance you need to be able to land.'

How did you come to meet Idi Amin?

That was in 1962. I was in Kampala and had contracted cerebral malaria and was very, very ill. I was unconscious for three weeks, when one day, just as I was starting to recover, I looked up and there he was at my bedside.

You were, I understand, the model for the journalist in Andrzej Wajda's film Rough Treatment. *And Wajda describes you as a man who can't sit still. You depart and then you return, tell a few stories and then disappear again. To what extent were you using your travels to collect material for the writing you would later do?*

No, you don't understand. I was there in Africa because I found it so compelling. I was aware that I was seeing something unique for I was there at an important historical moment – the liberation of Africa – when African nations everywhere were declaring their independence.

I wish I could convey what Africa was like. I have experienced nothing like it. Africa has its own personality. Sometimes it is a sad personality, sometimes impenetrable, but always unrepeatable. Africa was dynamic. It was aggressive, on the attack. And I liked that. Afterwards, now, finding myself in quiet surroundings, amid conditions of stability in Europe, I become bored.

I wasn't in Africa to collect experience. I was merely a journalist, working for an agency. It is true that I saw myself as a writer but I always had – as a poet, having been a published poet for years.

You're living in a country which, on the whole, seems to believe that it has a Marxist government imposed upon it against its will. On the other hand, you have witnessed a number of revolutions with which you have often shown a great deal of sympathy that were in the name of Marxism. Do you feel a genuine revolution is possible? Have you not seen too much to believe in the hope that a revolution offers?

It was in the nineteenth century that faith in science invited an analogous faith in history, that history had laws, that it could be known, that it followed a pattern. What we believe now – certainly what I believe – is very different. History is impossible to penetrate, and that is its great richness.

Yes, there can be revolutions, revolutions that begin in the name of justice, and bring about some version of just reform. Salazar in Portugal, for instance. And there are others which do not succeed. But I am much more interested in the mystery of history, why a revolution ever takes place in the first place. In Ethiopia, the revolution began because of the increase in the price of petrol. But the price of petrol had been increasing for years. Why suddenly a revolution?

It is easy to point to the parallels between the political situations described in your books and the political situation in Poland. The corrupt court of Haile Selassie suggests the corrupt bureaucracy of Warsaw; the mad, irrational modernization of the Shah recalls Gierek and the uncontrolled spending of the seventies. In your travels through Africa, were you aware of the Polish parallels?

In Africa, you find a population fighting for its independence, and trying to preserve its traditions to establish its national identity. But I wasn't looking for parallels.

Are you aware that readers here in Poland see the parallels and read your books almost as allegories?

No, they are not allegories. But there are bound to be parallels, of course.

What kind of relationship do you have with your readers in Poland? Or, to put it another way, is the experience of being a writer in Poland different from what you believe it would be if you were living in western Europe?

Yes, yes, I think it's a very different experience. I'll give you an example. Not so long ago I was invited to a town outside Warsaw to give a reading. It was scheduled to begin at five o'clock, and I arrived about half an hour early. But it was impossible to get in. The hall was packed. In fact, it was so packed that no one, with so many people squeezed up against the door-frame, was able to get out. By the time I succeeded in reaching the podium, I had been crushed and pressed and pulled by so many bodies that all my buttons had popped off. My shirt was torn, and I had lost my glasses. At around five-thirty, I began reading.

It's ironic that western writers, especially Americans, have always envied the writer living under a politically repressive regime, who enjoys what George Steiner has described as the 'muse of censorship'. Your work does not presuppose a muse of this sort at all. Even so, you have what few western writers could ever hope to enjoy – stories to tell, and a readership that's desperate to hear them. You could almost be described as a story-teller of the

*most traditional sort – a voyager returning with the stories of his voyage. I
am curious about how you made the transition from being a press agency
journalist to a writer. What made you want to write books?*

Again, my work as an agency journalist is important, because all my books
developed from the experiences I had. My responsibility was always to cover
an event – to locate the geopolitical story – and as quickly as possible send a
cable down the line with its details. It was straightforward journalism, nothing
more, nothing less. But once I had sent the cable, I was always left with a
feeling of inadequacy. I had only covered the political event, and not really
conveyed the deeper, and, I felt, truer nature of what was going on. And this
sense of dissatisfaction remained with me each time I returned to Poland.

You can always find two versions of my work. The first version is what I
do when I'm in the field – it's all in the cables, the stories filed. The second
version is what I write later, and that expresses what I actually felt, what I
lived through, the reflections surrounding the simple news story.

A press cable is a very conservative medium for conveying news. We are
always limited – by the number of words, by the time we can get on the
machine, by the money, by the information that the newspapers back home
want to receive. But the realities we face, especially in the Third World, are so
much richer, more complicated, than a newspaper will ever allow us to report.

What kind of story was not getting expressed in a newspaper?

It is not the story that is not getting expressed, it's what surrounds the story.
The climate, the atmosphere on the street, the feeling of the people, the gossip
of the town, the smell, the thousand, thousand elements of reality that are part
of the event you read about in 600 words in your morning paper.

Sometimes the critical response to my books is amusing. There are so
many complaints – Kapuściński never mentions dates, Kapuściński never
gives the name of the minister, he has forgotten the order of events. All
that, of course, is exactly what I avoid. If those are the questions you want
answered, you can visit your local library where you will find everything
you need – the newspapers of the time, the reference books, a dictionary.

*Your sense of inadequacy as a reporter is analogous to the sense of inad-
equacy many modernist novelists felt when they said that the demands of
the traditional plot or story inhibited the expression of the real story – the
things surrounding the story.*

Yes, that is what I am trying to express.

How, then, are you different from a novelist?

Ah, you have just touched upon an important point in my thinking. Twenty years ago, I was in Africa, and this is what I saw – I went from revolution to coup d'état, from one war to another – I witnessed, in effect, history in the making, real history, contemporary history, our history. But I was also surprised. I never saw a writer. I never met a poet or a philosopher – even a sociologist. Where were they? Such important events and not a single writer anywhere?

Then I would return to Europe and I would find them. They would be at home, writing their little domestic stories – the boy, the girl, the laughing, the intimacy, the marriage, the divorce – in short, the same story we've been reading over and over again for a thousand years. You know, the other day I was reading about the novels that won the annual French prizes. It was incredible. None of these books had anything to do with our world, our reality – nothing. There was one about an unwanted child, and another about a boy, a girl, the laughing, the intimacy—

Is it then that you find contemporary literature too self-referential, too obsessed with its own formal workings to—

No, it is simply that so much of our literature is so very traditional, even when seen as being avant-garde. And if avant-garde, it is only avant-garde because of its style – as if assembled in a workshop. It is never avant-garde for its subject; it is never caught actually looking out at the world. The writer is always looking over his shoulder, noting the position of his predecessor. Contemporary literature is a very private affair.

I am reminded of Joseph Brodsky's essay on the Russian novel in which he says that the twentieth century will never produce a genuinely 'Russian' novel, because so much of the literary imagination is dominated by the state – either in obeisance to it, or even in necessary resistance to it. Your work probably comes the closest to being freed from the constraints of the state. Its allegiances are to history.

I don't know. I'm not forming a manifesto and I certainly don't want to appear dogmatic. But I do feel that we are describing a new kind of literature. I feel sometimes that I am working in a completely new field of literature, in an area that is both unoccupied and unexplored.

The literature of political experience?

The literature of personal . . . no, that's not right. You know, sometimes, in describing what I do, I resort to the Latin phrase *silva rerum* – the forest of things. That's my subject – the forest of things, as I've seen it, living and travelling in it. To capture the world you have to penetrate it as completely as possible.

— But using story to make sense of this forest of things, to give it shape and coherence? For your writing certainly relies on narrative.

Yes, story is the beginning. It is half of the achievement. But it is not complete until you, as the writer, become part of it. As a writer, you have experienced this event in your own skin, and it is your experience, this feeling along the surface of your skin, that gives your story its coherence – it is what is at the centre of the forest of things.

The traditional trick of literature is to obscure the writer, to express the story through a fabricated narrator describing a fabricated reality. But for me, what I have to say is validated by the fact that I was there, that I witnessed the event. There is, I admit, a certain egoism in what I write, always complaining about the heat or the hunger or the pain I feel, but it is terribly important to have what I write authenticated by its being lived. You could call it, I suppose, personal reportage, because the author is always present. I sometimes call it literature by foot.

How is this different from New Journalism – the work of Hunter S. Thompson, Joan Didion or Tom Wolfe – who also put a premium on the first-person reporter?

That's an important question. And while I knew nothing about New Journalism when I was in Africa, I can see now that New Journalism was the beginning for liquidating the border between fact and fiction. But New Journalism was ultimately just journalism, describing the strangeness of America. I think we have gone beyond all that. It is not a New Journalism, but a New Literature.

Why am I a writer? Why have I risked my life so many times, come so close to dying? Is it to report the weirdness? To earn my salary? Mine is not a vocation, it's a mission. I wouldn't subject myself to these dangers if I didn't feel that there was something overwhelmingly important – about history, about ourselves – that I felt compelled to get across. This is more than journalism